How to Cash in on Distressed Real Estate in a Down Market

WHY OPPORTUNITY INVESTORS ARE MAKING THE MOVE NOW

ALAN D. POLLACK

with foreword by James Mencini

Alan D. Pollack

3401 S. El Camino Real Ste B

San Clemente, CA 92672

949-492-1151

APollack@sbcglobal.net

DeltaInvestmentGroup.com

Limits of Liability and Disclaimer of Warranty

The author and publisher shall not be liable for your misuse of this material. This book is strictly for informational and educational purposes.

Warning – Disclaimer

The purpose of this book is to educate and entertain. The author and/or publisher do not guarantee that anyone following these techniques, suggestions, tips, ideas, or strategies will become successful. The author and/or publisher shall have neither liability nor responsibility to anyone with respect to any loss or damage caused, or alleged to be caused, directly or indirectly by the information contained in this book.

ISBN: 978-0-615-49918-5

"Alan is one of the most knowledgeable real estate professionals I know, and he proves it in this book. The due diligence checklist alone, makes this book worth having."

—*JW Najarian, Founder, Commercial Real Estate Distressed Assets Association*

"Alan Pollack has the sharpest business and real estate mind of anyone I have ever met. He could have easily written something complicated and sophisticated for academics. But, instead, he has provided a clear, concise book that is a must read for the novice getting into the business and a great reference guideline for the most experienced. A must read for anyone serious about being successful in the distressed assets arena."

—*Kevin Perkins, Real Estate and Financial Consultant*

"Alan is the 'go to' guy for distressed properties."

—*Jim Shute, J.W. Shute International*

"Alan's review of the importance and detailed requirements of due diligence for distressed property investment is outstanding. He does not waste the reader's time with excess verbiage, but provides clear and comprehensive outlines and checklists for the serious investor. This chapter alone is worth the price of the book—multiple times over!"

—*Kathy Scheiern, Business Consultant*

"Alan's ability to identify relevant technology trends will help everyone in CRE."

—*Ronald Elsis, Geospatial Product Management Solutions*

"Alan has jam packed this book with the information, knowledge and guidance you will need, whether you are experienced or a novice."

—*JW Najarian, Founder, Commercial Real Estate Distressed Assets Association*

"A great read for an investor looking to buy in the REO arena. Alan is a seasoned broker with experience in the marketplace for distressed properties."

—*Sossi Crilly, Ticor Title*

"The timing of Alan's book is excellent. With private bridge lending as an industry standard in moving deals forward, now is the time."

—*Stephan Kachani, Lone Oak Fund, LLC*

"Cash in on Distressed Real Estate is an extraordinary … up-to-date inside look at the decision-making process of the distressed real estate market. I will buy this book for every one of my current and future clients. Fantastic!"

—*Jim Krieger, CEO, Abide Corp.*

DEDICATION

This book is dedicated to my late father (Jack),
who instilled in me a foundation of
"Do your best, be proud of your work, do it right, and do good."
Although my father passed on some time ago,
his teachings and my respect for his honor are with me every day,
and I've been blessed with his presence forever.

Acknowledgments

I'd like to extend my personal thanks to the many friends, family, colleagues, business affiliates, and clients who have welcomed my opinions, expertise in a changing market, and shift in paradigm.

A special thanks to my business partner James Mencini, who has been my peer and super-fan through all of our endeavors and challenges. His continued support, appreciation, and unwavering championship have been extremely motivational for me.

A big thank you goes to Donna Kozik, whose "you can do it" support and motivation have made my vision a reality.

Rick Itzkowich from Productive Learning and Leisure has provided a steady and supportive role to overcome self-doubt with a "get back in touch" foundation. Feelings are a powerful motivational driver, and my experience and training with Rick over the years have provided the confidence I needed to accomplish this dream and realize the vision of publishing my material.

A huge thanks goes out to my family—and especially my big sister, Susan Pollack, PhD, who is more than accomplished in her vocation, education, family, instructional practices, and encouragement. Her patience for proofreading and helping to edit this manuscript is beyond measure. Also, I want to thank my other brothers and sisters for their great support and encouragement. I'm hopeful that the writing of this book will provide an added inspiration for them to share their experiences and knowledge with the world.

And finally, special thanks to Carrie Rossenfeld for her patience and expertise in editing the draft and providing a final edit. For me, the start was easy. It was ambitious and had a purpose. The end was always in sight. But the middle—the editing portion—was the heavy lifting, so having Carrie there to move things along helped bring this idea to the finish line.

DISCLOSURE

IMPORTANT NOTICE:

THIS BOOK CONTAINS REFERENCES TO VARIOUS INCOME TAX AND LEGAL ISSUES, WHICH INFORMATION IS NOT TO BE RELIED UPON WITH REGARD TO ANY SPECIFIC JURISDICTION, INSTANCE OR WITH RESPECT TO ANY PARTICULAR TRANSACTION OR BUSINESS OBJECTIVE.

ALWAYS RETAIN OUTSIDE LEGAL COUNSEL AND ACCOUNTING ADVISORS. THE AUTHOR, ITS AFFILIATES, EMPLOYEES, ASSOCIATIONS, AND BROKERS ARE NOT AN ACCOUNTANCY, LAW FIRM, OR REAL ESTATE AGENCY WITH ANY SPECIFIC REPRESENTATION, AND THEREFORE ADVISE ALL READERS TO EMPLOY THE SERVICES OF APPROPRIATE LICENSED PROFESSIONALS IN ALL RELATED MATTERS.

THIS BOOK IS EXPRESSLY NOT INTENDED TO IMPLY ANY ASSURANCES WITH RESPECT TO THE NATIONAL OR LOCAL ECONOMY, REAL ESTATE APPRECIATION, PROFIT POTENTIAL, OR THE ELIMINATION OF THE ORDINARY RISKS OF REAL ESTATE INVESTING AND/OR OWNERSHIP.

ABOUT THE AUTHOR

Alan D. Pollack, President, Delta Investment Group Inc.

Alan Pollack is the founder and president of Delta Investment Group, Inc. He has been a licensed California real estate broker since 2001 and a former registered representative in the securities sector. Prior to the market downturn of 2008, Mr. Pollack specialized in commercial real estate, NNN, and tenants-in-common (TIC), participating in over $50 million of placements.

Beginning in 2003, he provided 1031 safe-harbor parking strategies as well as lifestyle-change and estate-planning strategies for his clients. His strategies are well suited for retirement portfolio balancing of self-directed IRA/401(k) as well as for passive real estate investing. During the 2009-10 market change, Mr. Pollack provided a transparent and equitable process of bringing off-market, unlisted distressed assets to the public market. He works with direct buyers, funds, and REITs to acquire discounted commercial and asset pools and tracked nearly $1 billion of distressed assets in 2010. His analytical tools include Strike Point Calculator© and Monthly IRR© for profit and risk calculations. He is a member of the San Diego Board of Realtors® (SDAR), National Board of Realtors (NAR), Realtor®, has completed several courses with the CCIM Institute, and is a member of several local, regional, and national exchange and professional organizations.

Mr. Pollack has recently been appointed to the advisory board of the Commercial Real Estate Distressed Asset Association (CREDAA), is co-chair of the association's Education Committee, and is a contributor to the association's certification and designation committee. He received his Bachelor Degree from the University of Wisconsin-Milwaukee and completed postgraduate studies at LaSalle University. He resides in San Clemente, California.

ABOUT US

Delta Investment Group, Inc. has been in the commercial real estate broker business since 2002, specializing in Buyer Broker relationships including 1031 strategies and Tenants in Common. Due to the distressed asset market unfolding in 2008, more clients favor unlisted, off-market assets over the traditional retail income deals with the potential to purchase at sub-retail, wholesale, and sub-wholesale price points. Taking advantage of relationships in the market with both direct and vetted sources, Delta Investment Group now provides a proven system for investors to acquire discounted assets across all commercial sectors, bulk REOs, and custom acquisitions. With a solid process of written procedures and an industry system in place, Delta Investment Group can orchestrate the most complex of asset offerings, including direct and non-direct vetted acquisitions.

CONTENTS

Foreword 1

How to Use This Book 3

Chapter One - **Distressed Assets** 5

Chapter Two - **Market Valuation** 11

Chapter Three - **Notes vs. Deeds: What's the Difference?** 17

Chapter Four - **How to Get Started** 23

Chapter Five - **Get Your Deals Done Now** 29

Chapter Six - **Due Diligence** 39

Chapter Seven - **SFR and REO** 47

Chapter Eight - **Know How the Banks Work and Assess Assets** 61

Chapter Nine - **What Works, What Doesn't** 77

Chapter Ten - **How to Balance Risk and Reward** 83

Chapter Eleven - **Truth or Consequences** 97

Chapter Twelve - **Frequently Asked Questions** 105

Glossary 111

Index 131

FOREWORD

The purpose of this book is to help those who want to learn more about the change in the economic nature of the real estate industry's post-market downturn of 2007 and the collapse of the mortgage-backed security and commercial mortgage-backed security (CMBS) markets, the rise in the foreclosure markets, accelerated unemployment, and the economically challenged climate.

For over two years, my partner Alan Pollack and I have evaluated and tracked over a billion dollars of distressed real estate assets from failed banks, local and community banks, FDIC and sponsored participation, Fannie Mae, bankruptcy attorneys, distressed sellers, and REO pools. What we have found is that the industry is inundated with infidelity, misinformation, "broker jokers," greedy amateurs hoping to pull a fast one, circumvention, fraud, little white lies, and a host of other clouded and covert intentions.

Due to our extensive knowledge in this sector, we are often sought after for advice and updates on the real estate market. We have found ourselves mentoring and training both inexperienced and seasoned real estate brokers, opportunity investors, and those seeking to cash in on putting deals together as buyer brokers or consultants.

Based on our knowledge and experience, Alan felt compelled and driven to write this book to give the novice, the seasoned veteran, or just the inquisitive reader an idea of how to "cash in" on this opportunistic moment to purchase distressed real estate. Has the market reached the bottom, or does it still have some more room to drop? Interest rates for certain are at historic lows and will surely be on the rise, right? Whatever the answers to these questions, the information contained in this book can help you understand "How to Cash in on Distressed Real Estate in a Down Market."

This book may help you change your belief system and encourage you to search out the golden opportunity of cashing in on distressed real estate while the time is favorable. With that vision, there is a new opportunity for wealth building using distressed real estate as a hedge to the changing economy and opportunity investor.

I trust you will find substance and direction in the chapters to follow as much as we have enjoyed sharing our experiences and success in this new, yet familiar, frontier.

—*Jim Mencini*

How to Use This Book

After years of evaluating deals, notes, properties of all asset classes, and buyer and seller trends, in addition to conducting an ongoing assessment of the current real estate climate, I decided to journal some of the deals I've seen—some that worked, some that didn't. As my three-ring binder grew with research, articles, e-books, profiles, and just about anything I could get my hands on to read (and save), I decided it was time to share the wealth.

In January 2010, I was asked to sit on the advisory board of CREDAA (Commercial Real Estate Distressed Asset Association), and my role began to change: I discovered that I was a sought-after advisor on topics related to the current real estate climate. As such, I was invited to participate in panel discussions, and my company's inventory began to grow even more.

With the company's heightened visibility and activity levels, I would find myself mentoring dozens of consultants, agents, brokers, deal finders, receivers, and other professionals on a one-on-one basis. Even bank executives would contact me to discuss the pulse of the market. This was both a curse and a blessing. Sometimes the training would involve as little as a question-and-answer or two. At other times, engagements would evolve into long personal meetings, countless emails, and article drafting to address the more common situations in the real estate market. I became a teacher and an advisor. All of these events have led up to my writing this book.

The purpose of this book is to share with you many of my real estate experiences over the past several years and to serve as a training tool for those who are asking, "What's going on?" and "How can I get a piece of the pie?" in the current economic climate and real estate market. No doubt, the market is grossly fragmented, but where do you start?

The book has been designed to begin with the basics: a description of the market, explanations of the terminology used, and a discussion of notes and deeds—some of which is almost elementary. But learning the terms, use of language in the industry, strategies, creative structures, and problems with assessing and managing troubled or distressed assets is necessary in order to save time and money in the end. Most of the time people waste in the process of real estate investing is due to what they don't know, so I wanted to educate readers on the basics first.

The middle chapters contain step-by-step directions on preparing to invest in distressed assets, and the later chapters deal with what not to do, since knowing what to avoid is just as important—if not more important—than knowing what TO do. The book finishes with risk/reward balance, FAQs, a glossary of terms, and an index to make it easy for you to find or review specific information.

I hope you will learn from this book and use my collection of experiences and advice as an ongoing guide to help you become prosperous and wealthy.

To your success,

—*Alan*

CHAPTER ONE

Distressed Assets

Nearly $1.4 trillion in commercial loans is expected to reset beginning in 2009 from interest only (IO) to fully amortized loans (meaning principal and interest), thus driving many loans to sub-performing or even non-performing status. The difference between sub- and non-performing statuses is blurry, due in part to the lenders' modification policies and the level of distress of the underlying asset. Since distressed assets will soon become quite prominent in the financial marketplace, it's important for investors to understand what they are and how they can benefit from them.

Distressed assets may take on a variety of meanings depending upon who is defining the condition of the assets. For example, prior to the financial meltdown beginning with the failure of the securitized residential loan market in 2007, the word *distressed* was usually associated with the physical condition or economic life of the asset. With the financial crisis accelerating in 2008, the word *distressed* took on a more solid meaning: financially troubled. This could range from late payments, modifications and forbearance, and pre-foreclosure to propensity that the asset will be in trouble in the future, as would be the case with the mortgage resets.

Most people are familiar with the residential real estate market. A house gets listed with a local real estate agent and is then listed on a local or national multiple listing service (MLS). There's often an open house, offer to purchase, escrow, loan, close, and then the MLS is updated for everyone to see. This is called a *comparable* (comp), which is used to price other properties, and its information is used by appraisers and lenders. Unfortunately, in the current distressed commercial market, this process is not consistent, nor is it as systemized, which makes the commercial market fragmented and difficult to value. It also opens the door for investors to determine their own value. In the commercial market, platforms like Loopnet and CoStar provide a forum to collect sale and lease information that can then be analyzed for market lease rates, sales comparables, history, time on market, and other pertinent criteria that can be used to determine price and terms.

The common rule in commercial real estate is that the commercial market is always the last to be affected and the last to recover; thus, 2009 is the early stage of the cycle. As the residential market begins to hit a second wave of resets, modifications, short sales, and foreclosures, values will continue to drop until a point in time when the residential market will be on the rebound. But commercial markets are a bit more challenging to forecast because of such factors as:

- supply and demand

- absorption

- capitalization rates

- occupancy

- replacement cost

- labor and material costs

- job forecasts

- economic life of the asset

- capital markets

- alternative markets for capital placement

- other uncertain factors

Also notable is the flood of capital from hedge and equity funds, REITs, private placement (PPMs), syndications, and individual investors. With this flood of capital, there will be more and more buyers chasing the market with the anticipation of buying at price points below the seller's acceptable threshold. In addition, the erosion of value will cause the banks to hold the assets for a longer period of time, and it is expected that this will result in more bank failures and compression. Such backlog, often referred to as "shadow inventory," is expected to drive more inventory to the FDIC and purchases that were pooled for Wall Street to be marked up for institutional buyers.

Like other markets (e.g., the stock market, precious metals), real estate is cyclical. Most investors have seen the cycles of the '70s, '80s, and '90s, the rise of the Resolution Trust Corporation (better known as the RTC) and the demise of the savings and loan industry. The ripple of the more recent financial crisis is touted as the most severe since the Great Depression that began in 1929. The figure below illustrates the phases and why the distressed asset market is primed for investors to make more money than ever before.

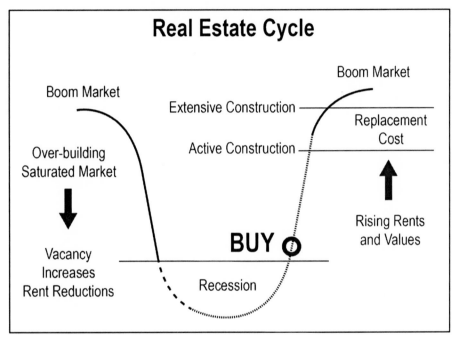

Figure 1: Real Estate Cycle

With the paradigm shifting to lender-controlled assets, a new strategy needs to be evaluated to optimize offer acceptance. In the traditional retail or commercial deal, the buyer makes an offer as low as possible with the sole objective to see how low the seller would be willing to go by virtue of a counteroffer. Unfortunately, in today's distressed and discounted marketplace, the lenders will rarely respond with counteroffers to test the "how low will they go" strategy. On the contrary, it is more effective to get the seller's attention with an offer that is closer to the strike price and to provide quantifiable evidence of the offered price.

The strike price is the range at which an offer may be considered or a negotiation begun. Factors to consider when determining a suitable offer may include: the cost and assessment of hard cost, reserves, cost of funds, cost of management, additional capital and tenant improvements (TIs), profit, cost of risk, and other factors that would result in a net offer. Providing such a schedule of expenses and liability is advantageous to include with the offer. An insulting offer may even disqualify the buyer in that the lender may not take him seriously for subsequent offers. Thus, on an unpaid balance (UPB) of $10 million with an expected strike price of 65 cents on the dollar, the proper offer would be $6.5 million. Offering half of that ($3.25 million) means the lender is at 32.5 cents on the dollar, and the offer might be thrown in the trash without response. A more proven strategy is to get within 10 to 15 percent of the strike price and negotiate based on due diligence, comps, condition, and risk.

Most investors are unaware that there are limits on the discounts a bank may entertain (usually less than 65 percent of the UPB) without concern about sending signals of distress to bank examiners or to the FDIC. In addition to limits that are presumed safe at about 65 percent, banks have a fiduciary responsibility to their shareholders to fight for every cent of the money due from a borrower.

Finally, to get offers accepted, it is helpful to know what makes lenders separate the amateurs from the serious buyers. Having a company profile, short plan of acquisition and exit, proof of funds, and professional LOI (letter of intent) are critical in getting noticed from the start and being taken seriously. Lowball offers are seldom countered, and oftentimes no response is the common response. It's critical to understand the bank's limitations and the fact that working within those parameters leaves the banks little leeway for buyer-expected discounts.

One of the more recent examples of working within the parameters of the bank's expectation and fiduciary responsibilities is an actual transaction that took place in San Bernardino County, California. A sub-performing construction note on a 77-lot fractured unfinished development with 18 standing units that were finished or near complete (i.e., needing only flooring or cabinetry), had an unpaid balance of $8.2 million and an expected discount to $6.4 million, which is about 70 percent. The sub-performing status was due in part to the fact that the bank had not filed the notice of default (NOD) and therefore was in the default status, but not in foreclosure. The project had a personal guarantee and collateral from the developer, so there was little incentive for the bank to take a large discount. The collateral had an estimated value of $2 million, which brought the net UPB to $6.2 million. At 70 percent on the dollar, that would net the lender approximately

$4 million, which would be closer to the actual current market value (CMV) and an expected buyer's strike price of an additional discount of 25 percent on the UPB. Negotiating by the leverage of the collateral and guarantee is a more strategic benefit that reduces the lender's losses and closes the gap between buyers and sellers.

Although here we are talking about the commercial market, these principles also apply to fractured development and the effect it has on other market sectors. A recent article in the *New York Times* focused on the impact of residential lots in the distressed asset sector. Over the past two years, in a number of markets stretching across the West—from Phoenix through Las Vegas to California—investor groups have been maneuvering to acquire finished residential lots that, due to the recession, ended up stranded without hope in a vast desert. There were so many unfinished developments of one size or another that the buying spree lurched along in starts and stops through 2008 with another great push at the end of 2009.

As a result, finished lots are being dumped back into the market at 50 cents on the dollar—or much, much less—by builders and banks that took back the properties due to loan defaults. In bigger developments, "investors have been buying these lots at 30 cents on the dollar," notes Nate Nathan, president of Scottsdale, Arizona-based Nathan & Associates. As of the beginning of 2009, California's Riverside and San Bernardino counties contained almost 30,500 lots ready for construction, reported Riverside's *The Press-Enterprise* newspaper. "If you take multifamily out of the equation, there are probably about 40,000 unfinished lots of standard, single-family-size (40 ft. x 90 ft.) in Riverside," says Nathan.

In November 2009, Nathan brokered the sale of 7,000 finished, partly finished, and plotted lots dropped into the market by two major homebuilders. Currently, so-called "money partners" are buying the lots and then doing off-balance-sheet rolling options with builders. That's because, for the publicly traded homebuilders, an extensive inventory of lots is considered bad business. "Investors are underwriting these assets to hold as unfinished lots for three to four years," Nathan confirms. By one estimate, most cities across the American West have about a two- to three-year supply of lots. By the time house prices recover, which optimistically could be as early as 2011 or 2012, developers will need to start building again.

With each passing month in 2010 we saw more and more buyers with large pools of capital looking for the bottom and expecting the recession curve to continue to move downward for a least a two- to three- year cycle, at which time the cycle will turn upward based on more statistical and analytical proof.

Summary of Chapter:

Distressed assets is a fragmented industry, due in part to its infancy in the current economic climate and inconsistency of monitoring closings, supply, demand, capital, and investor appetite. Over the next 5 to 7 years, it is expected that nearly 50 percent of commercial assets (including commercial, office, industrial, multi-family, retail, hospitality, and other non-residential properties) may be unfinance-able, in which case the distressed assets are expected to be around for a while. Understanding the basics through more complicated scenarios will allow the opportunity investor to be prepared for the change, both as the market continues to slide downward as well as when the market moves up.

"If we knew what it was we were doing, it would not be called research, would it?" —*Albert Einstein*

CHAPTER TWO

Market Valuation

If we were to start at the beginning, one would recognize that market valuation is always what a ready, willing, and able buyer would pay for an asset that an equally ready, willing, and able seller would accept. Herein lies the art and the science of that spread. As noted in the last chapter's header, "One man's junk is another man's treasure," and in today's market nothing could be closer to the truth.

Market valuation of any asset, including distressed assets, is part art and part science. Market valuation has several meanings based on who is sponsoring the cause. Just as a professional appraiser starts every appraisal with a purpose, using that same sense of purpose, we'll address this focus and provide some observations based on the current distressed marketplace.

Wikipedia defines "market value" as:

> the price at which an asset would trade in a competitive setting. Market value is often used interchangeably with open market value or fair market value, although these terms have distinct definitions in different standards, and may differ in some circumstances.

> Fair market value is defined as the amount in cash or terms reasonably equivalent to cash, for which in all probability the property would be sold by a knowledgeable owner willing but not obligated to sell to a knowledgeable purchaser who desired but is not obligated to buy. In ascertaining that figure, consideration should be given to all matters that might be brought forward and reasonably be given substantial weight in bargaining by persons of ordinary prudence, but no consideration whatever should be given to matters not affecting market value.[1]

International Valuation Standards defines market value as "the estimated amount for which a property should exchange on the date of valuation between a willing buyer and a willing seller in an arm's-length transaction after proper marketing wherein the parties had each acted knowledgeably, prudently, and without compulsion."[2]

Readers should realize that market value is not an exact science, but a concept introduced by individuals and companies as a business tool. Value is subject to both the seller's and buyer's individual perceptions and interpretations of parameters that they decide to take into consideration; it's unique to each person. It should be explained in this context because people pay what they want in spite of whatever advice they may get or whatever facts support their decision.

Also keep in mind that Wikipedia is written collaboratively, largely by anonymous Internet **volunteers** who write without pay. Anyone with Internet access can write and make changes to Wikipedia articles (except in certain cases where editing is restricted to prevent disruption or vandalism). Users can **contribute anonymously,** under a pseudonym, or with their real identity, if they choose. Therefore its value as an objective source is malleable and may be questionable.

As for local, regional, national, and international market value, considering that market price is what people agree to pay for something at a given moment at a given place, it is important to underline the importance of the time and place range wherein sellers and buyers meet. The "local and instant market value" of a specific item is exactly the same as the "local market price." And if several people want the same thing while there is not enough for everybody who wants it, market value and market price are identical. It is wrong to state that things have any stand-alone value, because value depends upon transactions. No transaction means zero value, whatever the value estimation or selling price expectation. When a lot of popular items in a place—for example, a great new condo in the best location—are almost sold out, sometimes people are willing to pay more than the asking price rather than spend time and effort to get it cheaper elsewhere. So is the paid price the market value or the market price? It's both.

How does one determine "overpricing" or "underpricing"? These two words are used to indicate that a price is too high or too low in regard to the expectations of an individual or a group. It is a matter of comparison to personal expectations and/or to some comparison tool—such as a chart, table, or formula—that is agreed upon and set forth as a common viewpoint by those people. Overpricing and underpricing statements are valid if related to the used comparison origin but irrational without such a basis. More often than not, these statements are purely emotional without any valid reference.

The term "market valuation" is commonly used in real estate appraisal, since real estate markets are generally considered both informationally and transactionally inefficient. Also, real estate markets are subject to prolonged periods of disequilibrium, such as in contamination situations or other market disruptions.

Appraisals are usually performed under some set of assumptions about transactional markets, and those assumptions are captured in the definition of value used for the appraisal. Commonly, the definition of "appraisal" set forth for U.S. federally regulated lending institutions is used, although other definitions may also be used under some circumstances:

> the most probable price (in terms of money) which a property should bring in a competitive and open market under all conditions requisite to a fair sale, the buyer and seller each acting prudently and knowledgeably, and assuming the price is not affected by undue stimulus. Implicit in this definition is the consummation of a sale as of a specified date and the passing of title from seller to buyer under conditions whereby: the buyer and seller are typically motivated; both parties are well informed or well advised, and acting in what they consider their best interests; a reasonable time is allowed for exposure in the open market; payment is made in terms of cash in United States dollars or in terms of financial arrangements comparable thereto; and the price represents the normal consideration for the property sold unaffected by special or creative financing or sales concessions granted by anyone associated with the sale.[3]

Most commercial experts have identified that the commercial market is still heading downward for a multitude of reasons, including:

- commercial resets

- retail and office vacancies

- job loss and unemployment

- lack of financing

- shift in demographics

- loans exceeding value

- cost of replacement less than the burdened loan amount

- lenders' desire to mitigate losses

- other market influences that affect the normal commercial flow

Breaking down the seller's side of the equation and considering that we are in a buyer's market, one would find more reasons to hold vs. selling into the panic. Sellers (and for the most part, lenders) continue to hold with the concept that we are at the bottom of the market and the period of hold will be offset with the flood of cash buyers who also feel we may have reached the bottom.

More and more investors are looking for the "bottom," which is buying an asset (or debt) at the "sub-" or "sub-sub" wholesale value. Sub-wholesale means under retail, while sub-sub wholesale usually involves an institution or large purchaser who then breaks the assets down into the wholesale market. The buyer in a sub-sub market might be direct to the FDIC, sponsor, bank, or other source close to the initial provider. Common other bottom indicators are:

1. Non-performing residential second notes are at 5 cents on the dollar.

2. Non-performing first commercial notes are at 20 cents on the dollar.

3. Performing first residential pools are at 50 to 70 cents on the dollar.

4. Performing first commercials are at 60 to 80 cents on the dollar.

5. Land notes are at more than 20 to 40 cents on the dollar.

6. Credit card debt is at more than 1 to 2 cents on the dollar.

7. Non-performing "junk" assets (cars, planes, boats, yachts, toys) are at more than 10 to 30+ cents on the dollar.

Even if you have been performing valuations for clients for years, what the banks and asset managers want is different. A broker price opinion (BPO) is not an appraisal; you don't have to base the valuation price upon closed sales. Talk to any banker or asset manager and you will discover that BPO and current market value (CMV) are all over the map. There is no consistency. The first thing you will do for a bank or asset manager is complete a BPO. If you are too high, you won't get the sale. If you are too low, you won't get the listing. Times have changed and you need to know how to value *distressed* assets in order to get business.

As mentioned in the previous chapter, nearly $1.4 trillion of commercial loans were expected to reset beginning in 2009 from interest-only (also referred to as IO) to fully amortized loans meaning principal and interest, and thus driving many loans to sub-performing or even non-performing status. The difference between sub- and non-performing status is grey due in part to the lender's modification policies and the level of distress of the underlying asset.

During the more recent periods of economic distress, the valuation of distressed assets has become more challenging and confusing in that values have to be normalized to today's market, economic value, and write-down of loan value, and repriced to today's replacement value, as well as a myriad of other variables not seen in previous years. The banks are holding on while the market slows down in declining values, hoping its losses will be less as time goes on. Many banks may not have the luxury of time to keep the asset, and therefore a current markdown may be the most efficient disposition. Market valuation is not the same as investor valuation. An appraisal is nothing more than an option backed by assumptions and evidence, but is not necessarily the actual value to an opportunity or owner/user investor.

Summary of Chapter:

Market valuation is the method by which a price is determined for a willing seller and a willing buyer to complete a transaction. Many factors determine the gap and timing of such a transaction. Markets are also dependent upon absorption, which means the higher the demand, the fewer vacancies, and thus a stable market. The more vacancies a building has and the higher the completion, the lower the lease rates. When lease rates are lower, the value for returns and IRR goes down, and thus the price points go down as well. Add to this the limitations of conventional financing and the number of available buyers is then reduced. For the opportunistic investor, the market shift provides a scenario for purchasing at values in the low end of the continuum.

References:

1. Wikipedia: en.Wikipedia.org/wiki/Market Value.

2. IVS 1 - Market Value Basis of Valuation, Seventh Edition.

3. *Federal Register* 55, no. 163 (August 22, 1990). This definition has also been adopted by the International Association of Assessing Officials for tax assessment purposes.

"Failure to recognize possibilities is the most dangerous and common mistake one can make." —*Mae Jamison, astronaut*

CHAPTER THREE

Notes vs. Deeds: What's the Difference?

Some investors are more comfortable with deeds. Some of the more sophisticated investors prefer notes. Each has its risk and rewards. Often it comes down to the security or rights of ownership.

A *note* is a legal promise to pay a debt, usually secured by a recorded security instrument, to notify all parties and public acknowledgement of the indebtedness. In some states the security is a "trust deed," and in others it's referred to as a "mortgage."

A *deed*, on the other hand, is a legal interest in the asset. Depending upon the position and priority, the interest could be senior, meaning there is no other interest other than property taxes in most cases. The "deeded interest" may be junior in nature, meaning there is some other interest (deed) in a priority position, and therefore the junior interest is subject to and must comply with whatever that senior interest has recorded with all terms and conditions recorded first, and thus superior.

Even experienced investors and brokers are sometimes confused as to which investment offers the best value in today's economic time: notes or deeds.

However, most investors are well familiar with deeded ownership. Deeds:

1. Provide rights and obligations (e.g., the right to lease, occupy, leverage, exchange, collect rent, maintenance).

2. Provide typical valuation based on cap rate, cash flow, loan to value (LTV), leverage, and rights of title.

3. Are subject to senior liens, property tax, HOA, mechanics liens, etc.

4. Are encumbered in title by junior and subsequent liens.

5. Allow split benefits including TIC, land lease, and title share (e.g., joint, community property, life estate).

6. Ownership is insured by title insurance to warrant ownership.

7. Provide for 1031 exchange and tax benefits.

8. Discount opportunities, REO (range from >.50-.70+ on current value), lease/options, etc.

Notes are the secured interest on real estate (unsecured on personal debt, e.g., credit cards). Notes differ from deeded ownership in that they provide other options for today's discount-focused investor; options for acquisition and exit strategies adapt more to today's capital market. The general guidelines for discounts are as follows:

1. Performing first residential pools are at 50-70 cents on the dollar.

2. Performing first commercials are at 60-80 cents on the dollar.

3. Non-performing residential second notes are at 5 cents on the dollar.

4. Non-performing first commercial notes are at 20 cents on the dollar.

5. Land notes are greater than 20-40 cents on the dollar.

6. Credit card debt is greater than 1-2 cents on the dollar.

7. Non-performing "junk" assets (e.g., cars, plans, boats, yachts, toys) are at greater than 10-30+ cents on the dollar.

Strategies for acquiring the note may include:

- buy and hold

- foreclosure

- forbearance

- modification

- resale to borrower

- value-add and resell to secondary market

- discount to debtor with terms

Positioning for note investors is as follows:

1. Other than residential REO whose value is based on current BPO, notes are usually underwritten from the beginning at 50 to 75 percent of value, thus there is a built-in discount to the face or unpaid balance (UPB).

2. Banks may discount commercial paper to 75-80 on UPB for performing to 50-70 on sub- and non-performing assets.

3. "Loan to own" strategy is among the most popular of strategies for acquisition and exit.

4. REOs from the banks may not be the best discount as they are usually listed with retail brokers once they become assets of the bank.

5. Note buyer steps into the shoes of the bank as the note holder.

6. If there is a guarantee, it usually goes with the note, and some guarantors will pay to get their guarantee off the note, thus increasing the net yield and opportunity to resell the note to the borrower.

7. Notes have an internal discount in that the bank can turn assets to cash relatively fast at the lowest cost since the buyer usually pays the fees. When the bank takes the property and lists it, the bank is now the seller and usually has to pay the commission, thus eroding the net profit. Also, the bank will have to clear the title, pay the taxes, keep it insured, and wait for a sale to be completed.

Some clients have asked, "Doesn't buying discounted debt entail a high level of risk, especially on non-performing debt?" Since that's one of the most popular questions, there are a variety of opinions. Buying debt at a discount is much like any other investment or commodity. Buying at a discount provides an immediate hedge against risk. Buying at a discount (20 to 80 percent, depending on the asset) provides a margin for profit. Each note has a unique strategy to acquire or exit.

There is a risk/reward in every investment. One of the ways to structure the acquisition of either the note or deed could be in the form of a *single-purpose, single-asset LLC*. Funds are either for direct purchase or as a member of a LLC. The LLC owns the note or converted asset, and investors own a proportional share of the LLC, much like stockholders. The LLC has rules and controls to insure that the investor understands the risk, benefits, and payouts. Usually in a LLC or *private placement*, there are operating fees, and the next dollar out to the investors is either as return of principal, preferred return on investment, or profit share. No true investment can guarantee that nothing will happen to an investor's funds, but if the controls and expectations are managed from the beginning, then the risk can be mitigated and reduced.

Like every investment, there is a management piece. Whether you do it yourself or have a money manager, someone has to manage the asset. A debt recovery market of 20 to 60 percent or more is not uncommon, but rarely presented to the private investor. We use in-house and third-party asset managers who have expertise in asset management, loss recovery, forbearance, modification, property management, investor relations, and operations. Some investors will choose to acquire the note and manage it directly, in which case a company similar to our own Delta Investment Group, Inc. will provide broker services on the buy/sell side.

In the event that there is no senior debt, there may be no responsibility to pay off any underlying debt. In this case, the asset is the debt. We purchase the note intact with all the terms originally agreed to in advance by the borrower. In some cases, there may be enough cash flow or margin on the note that financing would increase the yield, and therefore only the note is the collateral. This makes the investment an ideal purchase for IRA/401(k) in that the gains are deferred in the retirement account and the debt is paid by the LLC.

Some investors are focused on "income only" opportunities. Depending on the strategy of the purchase and exit, the note will produce an income based on the face value of the note or its modified terms. Performing notes, of course, will provide a cash flow that is distributed based on proportional ownership. Nonperforming notes may require some modification or hold for an exit disposition, which may include selling to a secondary market, foreclosure, or resale to the original borrower.

From the beginning, the note will be managed as an asset of the LLC. There will be an escrow to document the acquisition. Either in-house or third-party asset management will provide monthly accounting of the asset, including income, expense, management fees, distributions, legal update, asset updates. The management of a note is much easier than a physical asset in that there are no tenants or facilities to manage until a foreclosure is completed, at which time a property management firm will be engaged as determined by management.

Self-directed IRA and 401(k) funds are sources of funding often sought after by SFR flippers (those who buy low and sell high—often in a rapidly-rising market—or buy a house that needs repair and fix it up before reselling), transactional funding, passive investment offers, and other angel- and investor-sought capital. Like other types of real estate or asset ownership, your IRA/401(k) can purchase a whole note, note in partnership, or as a member of an LLC. All the gains and profits grow tax-free until distribution, so notes make a great alternative to other real estate ownership.

Because liquid IRA and 401(k) funds are currently earning single-digit (2 to 3 percent) return, there is a desire to seek higher returns without the added risk. I personally would caution jumping into any investment that is promising double-digit returns and manage the expectations with a more conservative approach. Always seek professional tax and legal advice whenever making an investment decision.

Summary of Chapter:

Notes and deeds have different strategies for acquisition and disposition. Notes usually provide cash flow and security. The maintenance is the responsibility of the owner or tenant, and thus, for the passive hands-off investor, a note may be a more attractive investment. There is usually a cushion to the face or market value. Many opportunity investors seek notes as a way to acquire the asset at a discount since in distressed situations a "loan to own" strategy is the objective. Deeds provide ownership in title and the highest form of ownership subject to any obligations (e.g., taxes, mortgages). Deeds are an excellent choice for active ownership and decision control. It is not unusual to see a higher discount on notes than on deeds, since typically the note is at some discount to the LTV and therefore already below the market price. When the market price is less than the note face value (i.e., underwater) this could provide an additional discount in value and a lower price. Deeds are deemed more marketable since the evidence of ownership is the title and all the rights and obligations of the deeded owner. There are clear—and sometimes not so clear—reasons for each form of investment or ownership.

"The way to get started is to quit talking and begin doing." —*Walt Disney*

CHAPTER FOUR

How to Get Started

F or some people, getting started is the hardest part of many endeavors. For others, it is often the easiest. Distressed assets are really no different. No matter how you deal with getting started, understanding what is being bought or offered is the first step toward making a smart investment in a down market. Knowledge of the industry, economic climate, and resources are also critical elements of participating in this investment sector. The entire mission of this book is to give a road map to real estate investing during a changing time in the U.S. real estate market.

Until the recent financial downturn, *distressed* referred to physical or economically depressed assets. In more recent times, the word refers primarily to the *financial* condition, not necessarily the physical condition level or obsolescence. The financial condition of an asset may include:

1. Performing notes (PN) that may have underlying exposure. For example, now that tourism is down, the forecast for current borrowers in the hotel market to meet debt obligations is questionable. There is a general discount as well as a specific discount. The general discount range for performing assets is usually 80 to 85 cents on the dollar; residential real estate discounts are less, due in part to the velocity, lower unit prices, and lower interest rates. Residential also has more government restrictions and is therefore limited to terms variations that are more common in the commercial sector.

2. Sub- and non-performing notes (NPN or NPL). These notes are no longer assets to the bank, but have now become liabilities in that there were little or no payments being made, or they are in foreclosure. The general discount is usually 50 to 75 cents on the dollar, sometimes less if highly exposed to liabilities.

Short pay is a term in the commercial industry that means the bank will seek to have the borrower sign a deed in lieu and take an amount less than what is owed. In the residential market, this is more commonly called a short sale. The concept is the same in that the borrower sponsors the offer to the lender to settle for less than the encumbrances. This is done to minimize the chances for the borrower to stall, file a Chapter 11 bankruptcy, skim the income, or press the bank to go through a costly foreclosure. The usual discount is 60 to 80 cents on the dollar. The lender may still have recourse against the borrower, so the discount may not be as expected.

Bank-owned (REO) means the bank or note holder has foreclosed and is the recorded owner. The lender is not in the business of operating or maintaining real estate and will seek to sell at various discounts—usually 50 to 70 cents on the dollar, depending on distress factors such as liability exposure, comps, BPO, supply and demand, or the bank's financial condition.

I urge you to determine the level of experience, purpose, and method of acquisition, and to have an exit plan. In the great words of Stephen Covey: "Begin with the end in mind."

In the previous chapter, we discussed the pros and cons of notes and deeds. Sophisticated investors want the notes because they have multiple exit strategies. Due to the flexibility of notes and the generally greater discount, notes are a viable and often chosen form of asset acquisition. Since the banks are not the best managers of distressed assets, it makes sense that this form of asset is a likely candidate for sale. Additionally, notes provide a "loan to own" strategy, whereby the intent of the acquisition is either to be paid off with a net yield or modification of terms, or to convert the debt to ownership. These are all strategies to be evaluated prior to acquisition as a good, better, or best scenario.

Deeds, including short pay, REO, and pre-foreclosures, are for investors who require the deed for ownership. There are several reasons to have ownership recorded as a deed (such as a 1031 or "like kind" deed), including: the need to refinance, leverage the purchase, or hold it as equity; the terms of a syndication; covenants; and exit strategies. Few know that a 1031 can be used for purchase of a "note" as long as the closing transaction is for the "deed"—that is, short pay with deed in escrow.

Once the determination is evaluated between acquisition of the asset by either a note or deed, the next step is to determine which asset class to evaluate. Asset classes (e.g., commercial, industry, hospitality, multifamily, retail, development) each have their unique variables. It is strongly recommended that you fully understand your strengths and weaknesses on the different asset types. Seek professional advice from brokers, bankers, tax and legal professionals, investors, those who have been successful, and those who have not.

Distressed assets are seldom listed, for a number of reasons. These include:

a. The bank may not own it yet, as in the case of a note.

b. The bank may be only the lead bank and not 100 percent owner; therefore, getting all the participating banks to agree may not be easy.

c. The bank does not want to pay the fee. On a traditional commercial listing, the owner on an Exclusive listing agreement is responsible to pay a fee, which may reduce the net transaction to the bank.

d. The bank does not want others to know of their misjudgment and embarrassment.

e. Listing brokers are required to disclose everything known, which may include information of which the lender is not aware or for which the lender is not even liable.

f. Once the property is listed, it becomes shopped and viewed as a retail offering, which minimizes the number of investors who are interested only in non-retail off-market deals.

g. Discount investors do not want to work through mass marketing brokers.

h. Listed properties seldom have the sense of urgency that non-listed or off-market assets possess.

Once the asset class and form of asset ownership is determined, the next step is to have a snapshot or detail of the offering. Usually the process starts with the non-disclosure agreement (NDA), oftentimes called a non-circumvent (NCA), confidentiality agreement (CA), or mutual NDA (MNDA), which is used to prevent the dissemination and transfer of non-public information. It is also used to make sure the parties do not circumvent—meaning they do not "go around" the process to avoid paying a fee or getting a client who is not agreed to in advance. Since distressed assets are usually not listed under an exclusive listing agreement whereby the seller pays the fee, the fee is paid by the buyer/investor. This requires what is often referred to as a *buyer-broker agreement* or similar agreement where the buyer agrees to pay the fee. Disclosing the location, address, APN or other identity before an agreement is reached would allow the buyer rep or buyer to circumvent the procuring source and not be obligated to pay a fee. This is a paradigm shift in the traditional retail market and is required to keep the product flowing to investors.

Oftentimes the asset is not disclosed until the NDA is signed, due in part to the likelihood that there may be third parties (e.g., agents, other brokers, other buyers) who would share the information without consideration for the damage that may be caused to owners, borrowers, brokers, lenders and the like. In order for business to operate based on the intent of all the parties, an NDA is usually the first step in the process of building a relationship.

Oftentimes—and for the opportunity investor—the assets do not have the traditional broker package. Think of the dynamics of the opportunity investment process. The lender and borrower are usually at odds, if not by evidence, then by the simple fact that there is a lender and a borrower in trouble. The borrower is not meeting the obligations or terms of the lending agreement (note), and the lender has a fiduciary responsibility to its stockholders and the state and federal examiners for transparency. Unlike a retail-listed commercial transaction, the lender may not have updated financials within the past year, and the asset is not being offered by the borrower. This could actually be a benefit to the buyer in that identifying the lack of due diligence is a reason for a lower offer. Even if the bank has a receiver, asset manager, or property manager under contract, that does not mean these are documents that will be volunteered before contract. Appraisals are often done by the banks when an asset is in trouble; however, that appraisal is paid by the bank and is the bank's property. If a note is being purchased, that information would be in the file to be reviewed upon an accepted purchase contract.

Another misunderstanding in the distressed sector is related to buyer-broker or finder's fees. Since the lender, bank, or seller is taking the beating on the discount, writing down the asset, and taking the markdown, they will pass any fees to the buyer. Additionally, in most cases the bank or seller will not give a listing agreement, which does not mean that the buyer cannot request that the fee be paid by the seller. Since the assets are discounted to the market, so are the fees. For most transactions, buyer-paid fees begin at 3 percent, and larger transactions may be less while very small transactions could be slightly more. On transactions of larger amounts such as $100 million, the fee could go down to 1 percent, to be shared by all parties. This fee is usually shared by three parties: the seller rep, an intermediary, and the buyer rep. On rare occasions, there are only two parties, in which case the fee is shared according to a fee agreement. There may be referrals paid by the parties if agreed to in advance. Sometimes residential agents enter the market expecting to get 5 to 6 percent or a co-op of 2.5 percent, and this may still be available on retail listed transactions. However, since the buyers are working on paying as little as possible, the fees are also discounted, so on a 5 percent fee at 60 percent discounted, that equates to 3 percent, and thus the baseline. Hedge funds usually start their rates at 1 to 2 percent, knowing their purchase range is $20+ million.

As noted above, oftentimes a scalable fee structure is used since it is unlikely that the fee would be the same load on higher-volume transactions. Many brokers, representatives, and even referrals fail to understand the dynamics of the institutional transactions and discredit themselves with amateur fee structures. I have found using a declining-tier Lehman schedule with a modification to be the most acceptable and credible. The formula was first developed in the early 1970s by the Lehman Brothers for investment banking services. Before this, the charge would vary wildly from institution to institution. In some cases, the charges exceeded 15 percent. The Lehman Brothers created a formula to apply to the dollars in terms of total capital of a transaction, rather than a larger share of equity dollars.

Since the creation of the Lehman Brothers formula, many brokers have informally adopted it with some modification from time to time, since it is both fair and easy to use.

Most likely the first time you are exposed to an opportunity, you will discover the challenge of determining the players, the asset's value, and if there is even a deal to be had. Unfortunately, there are a lot of opportunity brokers as well as non-brokers who wish to jump into the path of opportunity and create a daisy chain. A *daisy chain* refers to multiple brokers in the deal. In a retail transaction, only the listing broker is entitled to a fee based on a listing agreement (exclusive, open, net, etc.). It is based on the listing brokers' advance agreement with others as to whether the fee will be shared or "co-op." In distressed assets where there is no exclusive listing agreement, the parties need to have an arrangement that is often termed "paper up"—before the parties reveal their buyer and seller. Rarely, if ever, is there only one broker direct from the seller who has the buyer. And rarely is there only one seller rep direct to a buyer rep. If that were the case, the fee may be shared 50/50. But in most cases, there are at least three touch points: a seller rep, intermediary (middle broker), and a buyer rep.

The fee is usually shared three ways (e.g., for a 3 percent fee, each would receive 1 percent. More often, however, there are referrals—the "I know a guy who knows a guy" kind of introduction). Many times, the referral feels that his introduction is the pivotal and dependent factor of the transaction and demands an equal share that splits the fee four ways, or further dilution. Unfortunately, one or two of the parties do all the work, and thus an unfair distribution is expected. To compound the problem, there is little if anything known about the distant seller or buyer, and seldom are these transactions completed. The market oftentimes relies on referrals to bring a property or buyer to the market. Where the scheme goes awry is the expectation that a pool-and-share distribution is best for all parties. There are numerous strategies and fee structures that can address the fees equitable to all, but it is doubtful that a split among four, five, or seven will result in a closed transaction.

Finally, to get the offers accepted it is helpful to know what makes lenders separate the amateurs from the serious buyers. Having a company profile, short plan of acquisition and exit, proof of funds, and professional LOI are critical in getting noticed from the start and being taken seriously.

Summary of Chapter:

The best way to get started is to have a plan. I personally complete a client and property request survey to identify the target asset, price point, disposition, and risk factors. Why do you think there are specialists—cardiologists, trial lawyers, professors of philosophy, or any other specialists in any given industry or career? Distressed asset opportunity investors are no different. It seems unlikely that a buyer for an office building would also buy SFR REOs. Have a target asset type and disposition in mind. Become a specialist in the asset class and market. It will be easy to change once you have a system down to migrate to another asset class if the opportunity presents itself. Have your funds in place so that when the right deal comes along, you are not setting unrealistic expectations or timelines to close. Finally, be prepared to perform. There's no substitute for the feeling of closing the deal by performance.

"If you know you close one out of 10, get the nine out of the way as fast as possible." —*Zig Ziglar, renowned sales guru and author*

CHAPTER FIVE

Get Your Deals Done Now

In previous chapters, we discussed the comparisons among America's current situation, the Great Depression, and the RTC (Resolution Trust Corporation) during the late '80s to early '90s, which shows that our economy is cyclical. Similarly, like any other industry or market, real estate has a cycle.

In the past 40 years, real estate has averaged seven-year cycles, although some are longer and some shorter. More often than not, the cycles are affected by political shifts, change in the presidential powers, and interest rates. The current cycle was the first one that may have been affected by the stock market in that the onslaught of CMBS and the crash of the subprime markets were the catalysts to a down cycle waiting to happen. In fact, with the acceleration of technology, world unrest, and global economic influences, most cycles are expected to condense and have an impact in shorter periods in the future.

So, how do we navigate the minefield of a changing market? Consider these top ten reasons not to waste time in completing your deals during a distressed market:

1. Buyers are buying.

2. Sellers are selling.

3. Fourth quarter is a good time for banks to get bad loans off the books for this year's write-down.

4. The banks are preparing to take back more distressed assets than they have since the Great Depression.

5. There is an expected $1.4 TRILLION of underperforming commercial debt that may not be financeable.

6. "Commercial is the last to be affected and the last to recover."

7. Timing the market is never a good strategy.

8. The net difference between buying when the market goes down another 10 percent vs. the "add-on" of 10 percent when the market goes up is 1 percent!

9. Cash payments and fast closing times (i.e., less than 21 days) get approved faster and with greater discounts.

10. Deals are getting done every day by those who take action. Procrastination is a penalty.

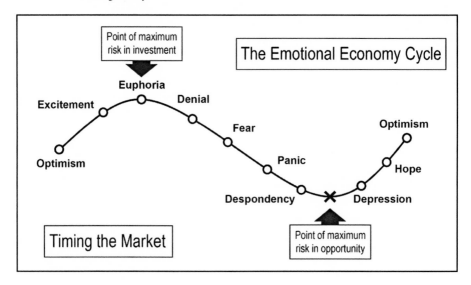

Figure 2: The Emotional Economy Cycle

Figure 2 above is an example of the psychology or emotional impact of the buying or economic cycle. To a certain extent, this could be converted to the selling cycle, although there are a number of life influences that take place on the sell side, including: health, death, divorce, relocation, change in tenant mix, vacancies, capital reserves, physical and economic obsolescence, and highest and best use. So, for this discussion, we will only look at the buy side of the emotional economy cycle.

Here's what you need to know to get your deals done quickly:

1. Have a plan.

We see dozens of line item offers every day. Having a system or process in place to move when the opportunity arises is critical. We see some "real" or "experienced" buyers and investors take too long to engage, and in the distressed market the good ones go fast—often before they become open to the public. A buyer who takes 30 days before even driving to the site is not a serious, real, or experienced buyer. Days—not weeks—are the key to success in today's transactions.

2. Be professional.

It's not just hitting the price point that makes deals happen. It takes professional elements to make deals go smoothly from the beginning, including: rapport, honesty, integrity, capacity and proof of performance, a professional image, respect, and remembering that the other person has both an agenda and a job to do. Use a professional document when making your offer, keep the due diligence periods as short as possible, and above all other factors, perform to the agreed-upon terms.

3. Have your cash or lending lined up in advance.

The days of "tying up the property" and then looking for someone to assign for a spread (the profit difference in a transaction) or resell (also known as "flipping") are gone. In addition, attempting to do zero-down deals on distressed offerings is a waste of time. If there's equity in the asset, a short sale or short pay on commercial will be equally as hard, so come with cash and have your financing lined up in advance. Some banks are financing the sale of notes and deeds, but not zero down. To use an analogy from renowned investor Warren Buffet, they will require "skin in the game." When dealing with borrowers or deeded non-bank sellers who may be motivated, you will need to show some benefit for them, not just a big payday in the future. There are numerous bridge and asset lenders who need to spend their money, since the preferred offering to their investors depends on lending money, not parking in bonds and T-bills.

4. Be able to perform in a shorter time frame.

Long due diligence is one of the major reasons that deals fall out. The seller gets tired and impatient while costs continue to be a pressure. The longer it takes, the more likely it will fall out and not close. The banks know this, and therefore the faster the close, the more discounts that can be negotiated.

Write a professional offer or letter of intent (LOI). Surprisingly, most buyers, even those who have been in the business for many years, either don't have a professional LOI form or think a cover letter is sufficient to convey the intent and make an offer. We've seen both sides of the spectrum and can tell you a professional LOI format is the best way to set the tone and capacity to perform. You never get a second chance to make a good first impression. Be sure to include clearly: who, what, when and where. Specify the price, deposit, due diligence time, punch list of due diligence items, specific date to close, fees, and disclosures.

5.   Have a personal or company profile available and attach it to the offer.

Sounds like a no-brainer, but rarely do we see or hear of buyers having a profile ready to include. We use this small value-add as a differentiator to the bank asset managers (or bankruptcy court) and receivers to improve our image. This could be a personal profile or strictly about the company, but of course has to be in concert with the asset and the offer. *Company* profiles have more impact than personal ones, but they can include the personal aspect of those accomplishments. Be sure to include a historical snapshot, as well as content that demonstrates the capacity to perform (e.g., volume, sales, size of projects, finance capacity, awards, and associations).

6.   Make sure proof of funds (POF) is verifiable and convertible to hard POF within 24 hours.

A POF is exactly that: proof of funds to close the deal. A POF is not a letter to yourself with a phony name and P.O. Box. You may be laughing at that statement, but it happens. The stronger your POF (bank statement, broker statement, third-party verifiable source), the more the offer will be viewed as serious and demonstrating capacity to perform. A strong and clear statement may also warrant a larger discount in that you are perceived as a ready, willing, and capable buyer. Put yourself behind the desk and see if you would be more likely to take the deal to your chairman of the board with the written evidence demonstrating your ability to perform.

7. Don't lowball.

Like any other buy/sell transaction, there is a price the buyer is willing to pay and a price the seller is willing to accept. Arbitrarily throwing a number at a deal is fruitless. If you were to go into a Mercedes dealership and offer 50 cents on the dollar, I suggest you may have to visit every dealer in town to figure out that the price point is not 50 cents. (On the other hand, you may be able to find a private owner who will take less than the dealer for a variety of reasons. Also, the car comparison is based on a commodity transaction in that there is an open market for buyers and sellers.)

On the distressed asset side, however, the price point is based on the seller's capacity to take a loss or be convinced with hard evidence (e.g., independent appraisals, list of mechanic's liens, relative cost of defending in bankruptcy court, cost to complete, or comps) to warrant a price less than par.

Here's the rule of thumb for engaging with an acceptable offer: Aside from the terms or other leverage, use a strike price of 10 to 15 percent to the range of value. For example, a non-performing commercial loan on a multifamily property might be 75 to 80 cents, since these are the easiest to get financing—DSCR (debt service cover ratio; sometimes DCR) is usually 1.0 to 1.15, and multifamily properties are highly desirable assets. A strike price of 65 to 70 cents might open the range, but a 50-cent offer is a closed door. Remember, an insulting offer will not only be rejected without a counter offer, but any subsequent offers will be tainted with lack of serious intent, and higher offers may even be rejected. Contrary to public belief, the banks (and FDIC) are in business to protect their shareholders and make money. Taking exorbitant discounts is not a recipe for a successful business plan. (See Figure 3 for a detailed financial example of the DSCR model.)

Income and Expense Example Target Price to Cap Rate		
Purchase & Acquisition Price (Cap Rate)	6,120,000	8.6%
Gross Income	1,000,000	100.0%
Less: Vacancy	50,000	5.0%
Add: Other Income	5,000	0.5%
Gross Effective Income	955,000	95.5%
Expenses	429,750	45.0%
Net Operating Income (NOI)	525,250	55.0%
Value at Cap Rate	7,503,571	7.0%
Value at Cap Rate	6,565,625	8.0%
Value at Cap Rate	5,836,111	9.0%
Value at Cap Rate	5,252,500	10.0%

Cash Flow w/o Debt		
Purchase & Acquisition Price (Cap Rate)	6,120,000	8.6%
Gross Income	1,000,000	100.0%
Less: Vacancy	50,000	5.0%
Add: Other Income	5,000	0.5%
Gross Effective Income	955,000	95.5%
Expenses	429,750	45.0%
Net Operating Income (NOI)	525,250	55.0%
Cash Flow Before Taxes 5 Yr Hold	3,527,773	11.5%
Internal Rate of Return (IRR)		11.5%

Cash Flow w/ Debt		
Purchase Price (Cap Rate)	6,120,000	8.6%
Gross Income	1,000,000	100.0%
Less: Vacancy	50,000	5.0%
Add: Other Income	5,000	0.5%
Gross Effective Income	955,000	95.5%
Expenses	429,750	45.0%
Net Operating Income (NOI)	525,250	55.0%
Cash Flow Before Taxes 5 Yr Hold	1,230,381	13.4%
Internal Rate of Return (IRR)		12.5%
Sale and Dispostion		
Sale (Based on 5 Year Hold)	7,000,000	8.7%
Cost of Sale	140,000	
Debt Service and DSCR Calculation		
Down Payment	1,941,000	31.7%
Max. Debt @ DSCR	4,179,000	68.3%
Term	20	
Interest Rate	7.5%	
Principal and Interest-Monthly	33,670	
Loan is Less of LTV or DSCR		
LTV	4,284,000	70%
DSCR Target	4,179,000	1.30

Figure 3: DSCR Model

Figure 3 provides the calculation and comparable to determine the cash flow and relative DCSR. Based on the cash flow less the depreciation provides a net cash flow number. After calculating the debt service based on the expected terms (rate, interest, and amortization) the annual payment is divided by the cash flow. If the number is more than the projected DSCR, then there is sufficient cash flow to service the debt. Each asset class has a tentative DSCR target. For example, multifamily is one of the lowest DSCRs at 1.10, while hospitality could be 1.80 or 2.00, indicating there is a higher risk. The higher the DSCR the larger the down payment to cushion the risk and thus lower Loan to Value (LTV) the asset will support. In the event the asset to be acquired is a distressed asset, it would be important to understand how the banks analyze leverage and mitigate risk.

Be prepared to back up your offer with evidence, even if it means exaggerating your profit. Having a pro forma prepare to address how the price was determined is in itself a mini business plan. Consider the asset manager your sponsor to take the offer to the president of the bank. Give him or her the ammunition to support the price point even it if includes a 10, 20, or 40 percent return on capital. There is a value associated with risk, but that should be supported by market and industry analysis, comps, and declining absorption. Pro forma should include acquisition price, cost to complete, legal cushion, resell or lease-up costs, permits, holding cost, taxes, and insurance. Upon request, we can provide a due diligence list which can act as a punch list to highlight the exposure and potential cost associated with taking over an under-performing asset, note, or deed. The more the backup, the better the chances that price and terms would be acceptable. This could include providing a schedule of the cost to complete, third-party reports, city or government notices, permits, a statement from the engineer for code changes, BPO (broker price opinion) or BOV (broker opinion of value), wrap insurance, cost of removal if the property has been exposed too long and will need to be rebuilt from the foundation, or environmental clean-up. A punch list attached to the offer to raise the level of liability or exposure is a valuable tool to lower the expectation of a par payoff.

8. Write, write, write.

Duh! Nothing happens without someone making an offer. Seems pretty basic, but arguably the number-one reason deals don't get accepted is because the buyer doesn't write. In some cases it may take more than one try. Asking "What will they take" is not an offer. It's an invitation to reject doing business in the future. Again, how is an asset manager at a bank going to take a verbal offer to the president?

Write a professional offer, within range, backed up with support and evidence, and close the deal!

Summary of Chapter:

The best way to get your offer accepted is to put yourself in the shoes of the lender or seller and narrow the gap between how each party will look at the deal. Most likely, all buyers were at one time sellers, and vice versa, so the other party's viewpoint should not be that foreign. Having a physical representation of the cost, hold, and exit—whether or not that representation is shared with the seller—is critical to conveying realistic expectations. Having unrealistic profit expectations or flippantly throwing numbers out is a sure way to be dismissed as a serious investor. Be courteous and respectful. No one wants to do business with a jerk, and if you have to ask what that means, then you know from which side of the net you're playing. Write the offer, work out the details, and above all—perform.

> "Exert control over the variables that are within your control and you'll improve the odds that the uncontrollable variables will work in your favor."
> —*D. A. Benton, executive consultant*

CHAPTER SIX

Due Diligence

D*ue diligence* is the process of verifying asset intelligence and mitigating risk. It involves researching known information as well as uncovering potential risks and obligations. Due diligence must be done on both notes and deeds, and in some cases the due diligence is specific to the asset class, title or secured interest, or nature of ownership.

Due diligence is both general and specific. General due diligence should be done no matter what. Specific due diligence gets down to the nitty-gritty, such as the number of parking spaces in compliance with applicable codes, environmental issues, expired permits, changes in the local building codes, mechanic liens that may survive a foreclosure, title issues, and countless other unknowns that may come up only after a change of ownership. Identifying them in advance can save you thousands—if not hundreds of thousands—of dollars. Therefore, having a due diligence plan specific to the asset is imperative.

I have found that due diligence is often the most matter-of-fact step in the acquisition process, and yet it is one of the most important. It will uncover the reality of the acquisition, test the honesty and validity of the offering, and determine if the assumptions for acquisition, hold, and exit will be achieved. Often, it is more effective to use third parties—appraisers, accountants, attorneys, brokers, title officers, physical inspectors, city officials, engineers, and a myriad of other professionals—to validate or test the assumptions and commitments, or even something as simple as Internet searches such as Zillow or Google Earth (in the case of real property).

Over the years, I've evaluated and tracked hundreds of distressed assets. Since most of the assets have been distressed, we've paid even more attention to details other than just vertical physical structure, income and financial analysis, land disposition (including zoning, entitlement, restrictions, encroachments, and easements), and other asset-class specifics. Due diligence will expose the risk and provide an opportunity to mitigate potential costs and risks in the future. Some assets are fractured—meaning not complete or absent a permit of occupancy, incomplete, dormant, or vacant—and may entail a higher risk and liability, or may be in some other unknown state. Therefore, a due diligence plan beyond the normal course of prudent evaluation should not be overlooked.

It's often difficult to find a starting point to begin the due diligence process, so below are both a general and a specific list of tasks and items that should be completed and present. The general list refers to all offerings regardless of the asset type or condition. Then, based on the level of final market condition, a more specific and focused checklist will serve as a guideline to make sure all the details are examined.

I usually start with a standard list of due diligence items that is included with the letter of intent (LOI), which sets the minimum standard of what my due diligence will incorporate. Virtually every asset will need at least these items; if some are not applicable, then at least I won't forget to ask.

General Due Diligence Checklist

Make sure you have:

1. ☐ Annual statements of operations respecting the property or asset for the past two years' rolling period and updated to the current year's end and through the month-end prior to closing. The seller's tax returns should also be provided to reconcile with the seller's representation, and the price adjusted according to actual income and expenses verified by purchaser.

2. ☐ A list and copies of all franchise agreements, permits, management agreements, employment contracts, service contracts, leases, and other contracts, licenses, and agreements relating to the property, including all amendments and modifications thereto, which may survive the closing date.

3. ☐ Copies of the seller's existing title insurance policies for the property or asset and a current standard form preliminary title insurance report, together with copies of all instruments constituting exceptions to title listed therein.

4. ☐ Current preliminary title reports or commitments for the properties from

the buyer or a purchaser-approved title company, together with copies of all underlying documents of record referred to, including, but not limited to, copies of currently dated surveys prepared by a licensed professional surveyor reasonably acceptable to the purchaser, purchaser's lender, and the title company. The survey should comply with the Minimum Standard Detail Requirements for ALTA/ACSM Land Title Surveys as adopted by the American Land Title Association and the American Congress on Surveying & Mapping, list all title report exceptions, and certify the following:

    a.   Except as shown, no portion of the real property(s) is located within a special flood hazard area.

    b.   The area and zoning of the real property(s) and the dimensions, square feet, and number of stories of all structures located thereon.

    c.   The number, location, and type (standard, compact, or handicap) of parking spaces.

    d.   The existing title policies for the property in favor of the seller and his or her lenders.

5.   ☐ A new ALTA/ASCM Land Title Survey of the land and improvements to be conveyed, together with any easements benefiting the property, prepared by a registered surveyor selected and paid by the buyer. The survey shall be directed to the buyer and selected title insurance company, and shall reflect the physical location of the property and all improvements thereon, together with all utility lines, parking areas, easements of record or in existence, and encroachments. The survey shall certify such matters as are required for ALTA/ASCM minimum and optional standards for urban surveys.

6.   ☐ A copy of any existing physical inspection report for the property or asset, prepared by a professional engineering firm, in the possession of the seller.

7.   ☐ Copies of any existing ASTM Phase I Environmental Site Assessments related to the property, prepared by a professional environmental assessment firm, in the possession of the seller.

8.   ☐ A list of all current employees at the property or asset. (The seller will permit the buyer to interview management, supervisory personnel, and other employees who will not be retained by the seller after closing, not earlier than 10 days prior to closing.)

9. ☐ Copies of the most recent two property tax bills for the property or asset, together with any and all assessments, and utility billings to the property or asset for the last 12 months.

10. ☐ Other documents requested by the buyer, including but not limited to documents necessary to: apply, qualify, and complete funding requirements; insure; comply with state, county, and local codes, statutes, and business operations; and any other document(s) deemed necessary for the buyer to obtain.

11. ☐ A list and copies of all management, maintenance and repair, and service and supply contracts, as well as other agreements, written or oral.

12. ☐ Copies of all fire, extended risk, liability, and other insurance policies, as well as a schedule of the premiums, current claims, and insurance-loss claim records for the past 36 months.

13. ☐ All plans, if any, and specifications in the seller's (or borrower's) possession.

14. ☐ A schedule of all personal property and fixtures.

15. ☐ Full disclosure and previous inspections known to the seller (or borrower), including but not limited to: physical inspections, mold, code violations, insurance request for repairs, tenant work orders, and zoning change notices or violations..

16. ☐ If the property or asset has been rented anytime during the past two years or rolling 24 months, copies of the last two years' financial statements, including rent roll, other income, expenses, capitalized improvements, debt service, cash flow, and owner's management expenses or draw. Utility and capital expense invoices must be available for reconciliation.

Specific due diligence is exactly that: specific. Based on the unique asset, classification, location, condition, timing, current codes in place, and a myriad of other variables, specific due diligence is used to address the finer points of the acquisition. The checklist below is a partial consolidation of items used in a variety of transactions and may help jog your memory or make sure you cover all the bases. By no means is this meant to be a definitive or absolute list—that would be impractical since no two deals are alike.

Specific Due Diligence Checklist

Check all items below that are required for compliance, due diligence, or under-writing, then cross-check them once you have acquired or completed them.

1. ☐ Original building permits and certificate of occupancy.

2. ☐ The most recent survey and site plans, including parking lot and easement details.

3. ☐ Any development plans for potential future project phases.

4. ☐ Any development permits or utility availability letters for excess undeveloped land.

5. ☐ Current easement agreements.

6. ☐ A historical understanding of who designed, built, and supplied the building systems. Are the firms still in business?

7. ☐ Original architectural and engineering plans and specifications.

8. ☐ Any as-built plans/specs, including electrical, mechanical, structural, and tenant finish-out plans.

9. ☐ Original construction contracts, including contact information on the developer, contractors, and subcontractors.

10. ☐ Asbestos and other materials testing.

11. ☐ Fire system inspection reports.

12. ☐ Fire extinguisher certificates.

13. ☐ Environmental impact reports.

14. ☐ Environmental Site Assessment reports.

15. ☐ Floodplain reports.

16. ☐ Engineering substrata, water, and geotechnical studies.

17. ☐ Aerial photos, if available.

18. ☐ Mechanical, electrical, and plumbing reports.

19. ☐ Copies of all prior appraisals.

20. ☐ ADA compliance issues. Is the building in conformance with applicable codes? Restrooms, drinking fountains, doors, and access should be in compliance with ADA.

21. ☐ The amount of remodeling that will trigger the need to bring the building up to current ADA compliance.

22. ☐ Ground-fault breakers installed in bathrooms, kitchens, laundry, and other wet locations.

23. ☐ The age and compliance of water heaters noted and checked.

24. ☐ Smoke detectors are UL- and local-municipal approved.

25. ☐ Is urea-formaldehyde or asbestos-containing insulation present?

26. ☐ Is the property serviced by private water or sewer service?

27. ☐ Is there any past and pending litigation?

28. ☐ Loan documents, including notes, deeds of trusts, closing statements, and debt/security instruments.

29. ☐ Any liens, i.e., delinquent taxes, mechanic's and lis pendens liens, mortgage, or deed instruments recorded against the property. A *lis pendens* refers to any pending lawsuit or to a specific situation with a public notice of litigation that has been recorded in the same location where the title of real property has been recorded.

30. ☐ The legal description in the title policy matches the legal description shown on the tax records and survey.

31. ☐ Any violations under the CC&Rs.

32. ☐ Any easements to which the title company might take exception.

33. ☐ Any encroachments onto adjoining property.

34. ☐ A copy of the insurance policy, including riders and the most recent risk assessment. You will need for the owner to sign a disclosure affidavit, including liability, casualty, and any other insurance coverage. You will also need a claims history for the property.

35. ☐ Request a general warranty deed from the seller at closing.

36. ☐ Regulatory risk assessed, i.e., local, county, state, and federal land-use controls, rules, regulations, fees, and taxes.

37. ☐ How many existing parking places are there, and is the property in compliance with applicable federal, state, and local codes?

38. ☐ Are any taxing bodies encumbering the asset (e.g., rental tax, property tax, transient tax, unpaid utilities)?

39. ☐ The most recent tax bills for the property.

40. ☐ A schedule of unpaid assessments, fees, or dues.

41. ☐ A schedule of service contract expenses due that indicates which contracts have been prepaid and which remain unpaid as of closing.

42. ☐ Other: anything else that might apply.

Once you've completed your due diligence checklists, you're ready for the next step, which is to summarize your findings—including assessing any financial cost or impacts for non-compliance. The summary or level of detail depends on how the information will be used. It is not uncommon to schedule all of the cost and expenses that may not have been considered or even known to the lender, seller, or borrower and include the schedule as an exhibit to the offer. This gives evidence to the assumptions and supports any discounts to which the purchaser is entitled.

Summary of Chapter:

Due diligence is the most important aspect of acquisition. It will not matter how good the price point is if the resulting asset turns out to be a "money pit." Investing time and resources into the due diligence process may very well pay off many times over in terms of risk and reward balance. Use third parties to ensure that you have not been swayed by emotion or perceived knowledge of the risk. Have a plan and checklists, and discuss them with your contractor, accountant, attorney, and lender, if there is one. You want to make sure you cover all the bases and eliminate as much risk as possible. Having a roadmap such as a due diligence checklist and a plan to address any and all associated cost and exposure is the only way to make sure your acquisition and exit strategy have the best opportunity for success.

One of the most useful tools to begin the due diligence process is a third-party software program called Property Archive, which can be viewed and purchased at PropertyArchive.com. Property Archive is a web-hosted, location-based due diligence and document-archiving technology that streamlines the real estate transaction process. The Property Archive technology creates secure, unique websites that store documents, maps, photographs, videos, reports, historical records, and other data related to specific properties. As the centralized location for property information, a Property Archive website provides 24/7 access—either secure or public—to lenders, potential buyers, appraisers, brokers, and all other parties involved in all phases of the real estate life cycle. For commercial lenders, the solution accelerates the gathering of crucial documents prior to offering a property for sale and completing the closing. Property Archive gives commercial brokers a simple way for their clients to visualize properties and perform due diligence online.

CHAPTER SEVEN

SFR and REO

S FR (single family residence) and REO(s) (real estate owned) are among the most exciting and yet stressful asset classes to discuss or with which to be involved. There are so many scams, unreal products, residential agents who want to make a quick hit, and other fallacies that it could easily take a second book to document the experiences and stories we've seen in the market in just a few years.

The old adage, "if it sounds too good to be true, it probably is" is an ideal place to start when discussing SFR and REOs. There are some common-sense realities that you'll notice immediately when dealing with this asset class if you're willing to stand back and assess the reality. The problem is that greed often gets in the way. The excitement of a real buyer proofing up hundreds of millions of dollars or of everyone wanting a piece of the deal can be blinding. But at the end of the day, maybe 1 out of 100 "buyers"—wait, that may be more like 1 out of 1,000— are real ... and that's being optimistic.

The first thing to understand is that an REO house is actually a foreclosed home. It may sound strange in the beginning, but let's look through the whole process of REO appearance. When a homeowner is not able to make payments to cover his mortgage loan, the mortgage holder starts its foreclosure process and, eventually, the house appears on a foreclosure list. In this stage of the process, a foreclosure auction is held, so anybody can attend it and buy the property being offered (usually held at the local courthouse steps). But if there are no buyers for this house, the financial institution (bank) becomes the owner of it, and the foreclosed home now becomes an REO property.

Let's start with some basic terms and definitions. The bank (lender) cannot list the house during the foreclosure because it doesn't own it yet, the borrower does.

At best, the fact that it is now public knowledge by virtue of the trustee recording, the NOD (notice of default) and subsequent NTS (notice of trustee sale) means the house is considered to be a foreclosure. If you buy it at the auction, you become the owner of the house upon foreclosure, which is evidenced by a trustee deed or judicial decree.

So what is the difference between these two terms? The main feature that differentiates REO property from foreclosure is the responsibility you take as owner of the house. The REO house is free and clear of the lender's claims, and any junior liens or judgments. Junior liens are recorded *after* the lender's position. They do not wipe out any secured interests that may have been claimed or recorded *prior* to the lender's position.

The standard for lenders is to get a lender title policy prior to closing, which would expose any obligations that would jeopardize the lender's known position. When the property returns to the bank after not being sold on the foreclosure auction, the bank takes the house and all debts, tax liens, fees, and all other payments connected with this property (but only those in a priority position over the bank's loan). This is the reason why banks have no interest in keeping REO property, as it leads to substantial expenses.

In most cases, the bank can't even cover its losses because when the borrower purchased the property, the price of the transaction was the cost (including loan and escrow fees) less the value of the purchase—much higher than the average price. Then the house acts as a security in a mortgage loan. In this case, even if the bank could sell the house at the highest price, it would not reap enough to cover the losses from this operation.

The best situation for the bank is to sell the foreclosure home during auction, and for the new homebuyer to take the title to it "as is." When the lender does not sell at auction, the lender becomes the new buyer and takes responsibility for all obligations connected with the property, but no financial institution wants this to happen. Some people who buy a house at the foreclosure auction think that it was a great deal for them. Of course, it may have been, but as a rule, expenses are much higher than profits from this operation. So in the end, the buyer may overpay for an auction house. It is much safer to buy a house on the market, which means gaining "clean" property without additional expenditure and exposure.

Short Sale

The term "short sale" is frequently discussed nowadays. For the bank, a short sale is actually a better solution, although there are challenges for banks to take less than what is owed on the house. Regulators, politicians, bank shareholders, and the like pressure the banks to stand firm on the obligation owed and do whatever it takes to get payment. The benefit to the new buyer in purchasing a soon-to-be REO is that they get direct negotiations for price, a clean title, time for due diligence or loan application and approval, and similar benefits to purchasing on the retail market with a discount.

For private real estate investors, it is much easier and safer to buy an REO house than to buy a foreclosure. Foreclosure auctions are risky, so it is better to leave it to professional real estate investors. These investors usually know which deals bring money and which don't, though even specialists can make mistakes.

Government Programs

With some government programs, there are policies and protocols of which most legitimate buyers are unaware, and they may get frustrated or dismiss real opportunities. For example, Fannie Mae (FNMA or Federal National Mortgage Association) has a structured process of property disposition. Upon acquiring the foreclosed property, FNMA will list the residential property with a local agent or broker for 90 days. In the event the property does not sell on the retail market, the property is pooled with other properties in the general area or by region. FNMA currently has 15 regions. Sometimes they will provide sub-pools by state if there are enough products to warrant adding a finer segment to the offering.

Product from FNMA and other government-sponsored agencies like Freddie Mac, HUD, and the Treasury are designed to provide low-cost housing and community development, so the product is on the low end of the scale and in need of light-to-heavy rehab (although some agencies are experimenting by offering homes "fixed up" in order to generate a higher sales price). Remember, many of these properties are abandoned, stripped of wire and copper, have missing doors, etc. They typically average $30,000 to $50,000 per door. (In states like Michigan, Louisiana, Mississippi, and other high-unemployment markets, the price may be $5,000 per door [a unit of measure in apartments or pool of assets].) It's unlikely that these properties are in the same neighborhood as where the investors live.

There is a resale moratorium of usually 90 days to prevent and minimize flippers whose objective is not to improve the community, but to flip dollars and often leave the situation in worse shape than if the property was delivered to a purchaser whose intent was to provide affordable, safe, and healthy home occupancy. FHA has placed a moratorium on this "anti-flipping" policy, but many banks still have this rule in effect.

Price Points

REOs are purchased by opportunity investors either to resell, hold for rent, or a combination of strategies. A general rule of the thumb for many REO investors who may be purchasing with the intent to resell is that the exit sale price must be in the 85 percent to comparable range. This is because if it were priced to the current retail market, the competition would be the home next door, where there would be no competitive advantage. Therefore, the acquisition price must allow for a margin of profit while at the same time a discount factor to sell. Using the 85 percent to comparable market and backing out the cost and profit, the model might look something like this:

Item	Ref	Amount	SqFt	$/SqFt
Market Comparable Basis		$100,000	1000	$100.00
Adjusted Re-Sale Basis @	90%	$90,000	1000	$90.00
LESS: Selling Commission	5%	$(4,500)	1000	$(4.50)
LESS: Seller Closing Cost	1%	$(900)	1000	$(0.90)
LESS: Light Re Hab	10%	$(9,000)	1000	$(9.00)
LESS: Taxes and Insurance	3%	$(2,700)	1000	$(2.70)
Net Sale Proceeds		$72,900	1000	$72.90
Profit on Acquisition (90-Day-Hold)	12%	$8,748	1000	$(8.75)
Net Acquisition Price		$64,152	1000	$64.15

Table 1: Example of How a Resale REO Determines Price Point

Thus, on the example above, a $100,000 house at the market comparable would first be calculated to 90 percent of the market. Some will use an 85 percent factor in that the price of the retail sale must be something significantly below the other houses that are for sale in the immediate area, although 90 percent usually is a fair strike point. Then all the costs are deducted, resulting in the net sale proceeds of $64,152 (or 65 cents on the dollar as the breakeven). Assuming a 12 percent profit margin for a hold period of 90 days would back-end an acquisition price of 64.15 cents on the dollar (rounded up to 65 cents). The annualized effect would be 48 percent (4 turns times 12 percent). This, of course, is market and condition dependent, but gives a simple illustration.

Be aware that condos, townhomes with an association, co-ops, and other housing communities may have a homeowners' association (HOA) cost, which could further erode the net profit due in part to an added monthly cost to hold. That is why there are more condos and the like on the market that need to be pooled with SFRs so they will get spread around. The price point on the pool should be adjusted (or weighed) for the added risk of ongoing monthly overhead regardless of whether it will be rented or sold.

Blended product is more likely to be less. In other words, the price point generally will go down when good and bad product is combined. The more selective the product, quality, market, and condition, the higher the price point.

The following table illustrates a recent pool of REOs with relative price points by state. During the due diligence of the pool for acquisition, several markets were tested for relative pricing of similar product and were found to be within pennies of the market swing. This is not to say these prices were at the high end or low end, just that they were within a range of prices at that time. Like any other fluid market, the pricing will change based on supply and demand as well as other factors of condition, community, employment, age, quality, cost of capital in the market, and a myriad of other variables that change from day to day.

Ref	State	Qty	As % of Pool	At Par Value	Price Pt.	Est. Value
1	AK	1	0.10%	$114,613	0.20	$22,923
2	AL	4	0.38%	$458,453	0.35	$160,458
3	AR	5	0.48%	$573,066	0.40	$229,226
4	AZ	41	3.92%	$4,699,140	0.52	$2,443,553
5	CA	164	15.66%	$18,796,562	0.64	$12,029,799
6	CO	13	1.24%	$1,489,971	0.52	$774,785
7	CT	5	0.48%	$573,066	0.55	$315,186
8	DC	2	0.19%	$229,226	0.27	$61,891
9	DE	3	0.29%	$343,840	0.49	$168,481
10	FL	233	22.25%	$26,704,871	0.46	$12,284,241
11	GA	51	4.87%	$5,845,272	0.38	$2,221,203
12	HI	3	0.29%	$343,840	0.60	$206,304
13	IA	3	0.29%	$343,840	0.38	$130,659
14	ID	12	1.15%	$1,375,358	0.52	$715,186
15	IL	57	5.44%	$6,532,951	0.46	$3,005,158
16	IN	14	1.34%	$1,604,585	0.37	$593,696
17	KS	9	0.86%	$1,031,519	0.45	$464,183
18	KY	4	0.38%	$458,453	0.28	$128,367
19	LA	5	0.48%	$573,066	0.20	$114,613
20	MA	10	0.96%	$1,146,132	0.45	$515,759
21	MD	58	5.54%	$6,647,564	0.50	$3,323,782
22	ME	2	0.19%	$229,226	0.50	$114,613
23	MN	17	1.62%	$1,948,424	0.50	$974,212
24	MO	5	0.48%	$573,066	0.37	$212,034
25	MS	3	0.29%	$343,840	0.18	$61,891
26	MT	1	0.10%	$114,613	0.50	$57,307
27	NC	35	3.34%	$4,011,461	0.39	$1,564,470
28	NE	2	0.19%	$229,226	0.40	$91,691
29	NH	4	0.38%	$458,453	0.60	$275,072
30	NJ	25	2.39%	$2,865,330	0.33	$945,559
31	NM	5	0.48%	$573,066	0.42	$240,688

32	NV	30	2.87%	$3,438,395	0.48	$1,650,430
33	NY	25	2.39%	$2,865,330	0.54	$1,547,278
34	OK	10	0.96%	$1,146,132	0.45	$515,759
35	OR	24	2.29%	$2,750,716	0.46	$1,265,330
36	PA	27	2.58%	$3,094,556	0.23	$711,748
37	SC	8	0.76%	$916,905	0.28	$256,734
38	TN	16	1.53%	$1,833,811	0.32	$586,819
39	TX	37	3.53%	$4,240,688	0.41	$1,738,682
40	UT	5	0.48%	$573,066	0.51	$292,264
41	VA	18	1.72%	$2,063,037	0.37	$763,324
42	VT	1	0.10%	$114,613	0.56	$64,183
43	WA	24	2.29%	$2,750,716	0.40	$1,100,287
44	WI	22	2.10%	$2,521,490	0.26	$655,587
45	WV	1	0.10%	$114,613	0.22	$25,215
46	WY	3	0.29%	$343,840	0.40	$137,536
		1047	100.00%	$120,000,000		$55,758,166

Table 2: Average Strike Price Point by State

In the table above, the aggregate discount is to $56 million, or 46.6 cents on the dollar. This is called a blended rate or blended discount. Individual sales or sub-pools by state could be slightly more, considering that economy of scale is priced better for larger volumes. Note also that the timing of the market will have a significant impact on the blended and individual pricing. The concept of supply and demand will be an equally determining factor on pricing during even the normal cycles of real estate, let alone during a down market.

Fees

Since the lender, bank, or seller is taking the discount, writing down the asset, and taking the markdown, they will pass any fees to the buyer. Additionally, in most cases the bank or seller will not give a listing agreement, which does not mean that the buyer cannot request the fees be paid by the seller. Since the assets are discounted to the market, so are the fees. For most transactions, buyer-paid fees begin at 3 percent, and larger transactions may be less while very small transactions could be slightly more. On transactions of larger amounts, such as $100 million, the fee could go down to 1 percent to be shared by all parties. As I mentioned earlier, I personally use a declining-tier Lehman Schedule arranged up front with the MNDA (mutual non-disclosure agreement) and fee agreement. The long and the short of it is that the greater the volume, the lower the fee.

Multiple Parties in the Transaction

Even traditional listed real estate has multiple parties, including: agent, broker, buyer's agent, and buyer's agent broker. It is not unusual that the fee is shared by three parties: direct seller representative, intermediary, and direct buyer representative. Representatives are usually licensed brokers, attorneys, or consultants. This is governed by state law and could include contracted consultants who provide a finding service, but do not engage in any contracts on behalf of their principals.

Be sure to check regulatory agencies for requirements for a license to provide a service. On rare occasions, there are only two parties, in which case the fee is shared according to a fee agreement. And, in the rarest of situations, there is only one person who connects the seller and the buyer. This is the optimum opportunity and prospect to close the transaction.

There may be referrals paid by the parties if agreed to in advance; however, in these cases what I have found is a greed and ego that prevents the real deal from ever happening. The deals most likely to be completed are done by direct buyers and direct sellers with any fees or points based on direct introduction and referrals in between.

I like to use the analogy of buying a used car. How do you feel about hiring someone to find, evaluate, negotiate, test drive, check the fluids, check to see if it had been in a prior accident—to kick the tires, so to speak—all on your behalf? Kind of a tough gig. Think about all that goes into evaluating the asset. Now multiply the stakes by 5, 10, 20, or hundreds.

The message here is that these transactions should be done directly between a buyer and seller, and everyone else should get out of the way. You'll know when this happens in that there will be a finder's or referral fees and not "mandates," seller's attorney, or "representatives" keeping the parties apart. Transparency is the key for a successful deal and closing.

Case Study One

A client of mine was offered a package in Southern California priced at $6 million or a discount of .60 to the current BPO value of $10 million. I told him that if it sounds too good to be true, it probably is.

California, along with Nevada and Arizona, are commonly referred to as the "Diamond States" when it comes to REO offerings. These states are not like other areas of the country. They are highly desirable and much in demand, hence the discounts are less than those commonly found in other states.

Contrary to popular belief, many local investors in these areas are buying between .70 to .75, holding and renting, or reselling to retail buyers for .85 to .90 on the dollar. Could they buy for less in these areas? Quite possibly, if they were purchasing inner-city low-end units that may require significant renovations and could acquire in the 55-cent range or less. As in many scenarios, it is a supply and demand balance.

Many of these successful trustee buyers know it is nearly impossible to buy a pool from a bank or FNMA or FHLMC. The reason for that was discussed earlier: typical prices are between .78 and .83 of fair market value (FMV) and are also tied into the current BPO. The BPO is the current market value done by a "for hire" agent or broker in the area, who determines the price based mainly on market comparables. Due to the price points, risk, and short timelines to bide, these investors bypass them altogether and buy at the trustee sales at the county courthouses. Obviously, you need to know what you are doing when purchasing at auction, since many times an auction is planted with "stalking horse" buyers to price up the bids. There are also professional foreclosure buyers who will bid up the price to get the amateurs out of the way; you can normally spot them at the courthouse steps talking amongst their peers. Be careful when you observe interactions that involve nods, winks, "tells," and associations.

Is It Real?

Opportunity buyers—or investors, as they are sometimes called—purchase 25 to 100 homes per month. They are doing so in Los Angeles and Ventura counties as well as in Phoenix and Las Vegas, as these have been the hardest hit for volume of non-performing modifications, accelerated 3/1 and 5/1 ARMs, unemployment, and the mere rash of hits to the economy.

Let's take another look at some of the more active submarkets like Southern California, which is packaged for .60 of FMV. Is it the real deal? Probably not, and here's why. Depending on the bank procedures, these REO lists are distributed to several local retail brokers whose job it is to help move these properties individually in the local marketplace. It is the fiduciary responsibility of the lender, bank, government agency, and the like to do everything possible to mitigate their losses.

Sometimes these same brokers will have takeout buyers already in place (i.e., a hedge fund) who will break out the most desirable areas (e.g., California) and offer this subset to their investors as a bulk package. When offering it to a buyer, they usually mention that they have exclusive access to the buyer mandate representing the bank. Translation: It is the broker who obtained the list from the bank and provided it to the service. The service is offering this package to you as a bulk sale.

A Process

Along with the "package" you receive, they include instructions for submitting offers. Most importantly, they tell you your initial offer needs to start at 60 percent of FMV in order to have a discussion with the bank, but that the bank always reserves the right to counter. So you do your due diligence by spending time ordering and paying for BPOs. You then come back with an offer at the minimum acceptable price of 60 percent of FMV. The service "submits your offer." The reason I use quotes is that most of the time, the service never submits the initial offer. It is an enticement to get the buyer to submit an offer that will never be accepted. It helps the service separate the real buyers from the tire kickers.

After three to four days, the service contacts the buyer to tell them the bank countered at .68, and that is the minimum acceptable price, but the bank still reserves the right to counter again. Although you are not too pleased with the delay in responding, you decide to recheck your numbers and determine that .68 may still be a good deal and agree. Now the service tells you that in order to submit the second offer, you need to accompany it with a proof of funds, usually made out to the bank.

Here's a behind-the-scenes look at what happens after your "second offer" is submitted:

1. The service takes your POF directly to the bank and attempts to negotiate a bulk purchase with the service as the buyer at 60 to 63 percent. They need

your POF to get the bank to authorize the sale and issue the purchase agreement. The service is attempting to double close and sell it to you at .68 and keep the spread minus closing costs.

2. The bank responds by saying that these properties were not authorized as a bulk transaction but on a per-asset offer basis.

3. The service believes they have the financial leverage to negotiate a better price since they are buying quantity with millions of dollars. The bank should be grateful to get these properties off their books quickly.

4. The bank responds again, saying that it is not an authorized bulk sale and that if they want to buy, they have to make an offer on a per-asset basis starting at the original bank price of .80, which is usually the starting point with a bank for California REOs.

5. After some back and forth, the service realizes they won't be able to get the package at their pricing. They come back to the buyer with another counteroffer at .80. They will gladly take you directly into the bank, but you will have to pay them plus three points if you decide to move forward. At this point, the service is attempting to salvage the deal by brokering it.

6. This is unacceptable, and the buyer pulls out of the transaction.

Many of you will ask, "How do you know this?" Well, I have been on the receiving end several times with these types of transactions when I first started out with REOs. I also spoke extensively with authorized bank REO brokers as well as a few bank asset managers who confirmed this off the record. I have yet to see a successful transaction structured this way.

One of the best ways to obtain REO properties is through the trustee services who buy directly at the auction on behalf of my buyers. Some banks will pull the tape away if they find these groups flipping without actually having the means to perform, which is why there is usually an application process. They will then not accept offers from these groups. The banks prefer to deal with holding companies, regulators, and vetted funds instead of street vendors who call them 40 times a day to see if they have a tape to distribute.

Case Study Two

We had a company in Orange County, California, approach us saying that they were the direct seller. They provided an LOI and soft POF, which would be verified upon acceptance of the LOI and delivery of the BPO tape … which never happened. They also wanted the hard POF and evidence of an open escrow for 10 percent. Then they said they had a buyer willing to pay 4 cents more than our signed and executed agreement.

The long and short of it was that this was always going to be a double escrow. They were too embarrassed or dishonest to be upfront. By the way, many buyers and funds will still do business with a double escrow if it is transparent and not grossed up more than 1 point. Our buyer has proofed up $100 million in hard funds and continues to look for direct, transparent, equitable deals. They are realistic at blended discount to 64 cents on the dollar in California, so that's not the problem.

Anyone who uses the word "billions" is bogus. Deals this size are done over cocktails at lunch by the Wall Street players, so when we hear that the buyers or sellers have done deals in the "B," we just say thank you and move on. Last, no one is going to get 3 points on $100 million. That is just a gross-up ploy and signals that they are a daisy chain. Do the math: 3 points on 60 cents is 5 percent. That could be more than the profit buyer with the money may make on the deal, so why would they pay you the lion's share of the profit they expect to make?

This is one of my favorite scams for which to be on the lookout. It's the "direct to the seller, really" approach. Not that there aren't real sellers, lenders, and banks that must move non-profitable assets, but the caveat here is that there are buyers under contract who tout that they are the owner of the tape or pool, when in fact they may be the buyer under contract and intend either to assign or close concurrently with the final buyer's funds. Since the tape or pool may be under contract or even in an escrow, they are not the direct and deeded seller and will rarely disclose that. Unless their name is on title, they are not the direct seller. If the assets are being sold by a servicer, then there would be no problem in getting a letter of authority (LOA) from them that they indeed represent under a contract to liquidate the assets.

Summary of Chapter:

Like many experiences in life, such as riding a bike, one sometimes has to learn by doing. The benefit of learning about the experiences of others is that you can be on the lookout for those who will waste your time, credibility, resources, and jerk you around. Ask for a Letter of Authorization (LOA) from the selling source, if not the actual bank, lender, or servicer. Beware of gross-ups and daisy chains as these are the first red flag. Beware of blind LOI and hard POF: they will be shopped using the buyer's funds and credibility almost like a free loan, so I say, "Don't do it." There is a legitimate and professional process, so beware of covert, non-transparent, un-vetted, and "you proof up first" kind of protocols. Also beware of attorneys who profess they are under contract to proof up funds without providing a LOA. If they or anyone else is "authorized," then it should not be a problem to produce such authorization. Bottom line: Although SFR REOs is one of them most exciting and profitable segments in the distressed asset sector, it can also be one of the most challenging and costly for those who take shortcuts or submit to unconventional purchase processes.

"Every one minute you spend in planning will save you at least three minutes in execution." —*Crawford Greenwald, author*

CHAPTER EIGHT

Know How the Banks Work and Assess Assets

An entire book can be devoted to the subject of the banking industry's ever-changing landscape in today's economic climate. Aside from the Great Depression (1929-1939), the only other notable challenge in the history of U.S. banking was the Resolution Trust Corporation (RTC) in the late 1980s and early 1990s, which collapsed the savings and loan industry. For some, the impact of this collapse (and its resultant opportunity) makes it feel like yesterday. In 2010, there were 156 bank failures, and the forecast is that the number of bank failures in 2011 will increase.

There are many opinions and expert testimony on what caused the problems and how we got here—but frankly, that's old news. Based on a variety of changes in the residential, commercial, and mortgage industries, combined with the collapse of mortgage-backed securities, and economic and political changes in 2007-08, the market is prime for pushing product into the private sector at significant discounts. The graph below, provided by industry analytics leader Real Capital Analytics, is a visual representation of the historical changes and current climate of the market through third quarter 2010. The broad-brush vision of the company will target the acquisition of discounted distressed real estate assets with a predefined repositioning plan in accordance with the company's guidelines.

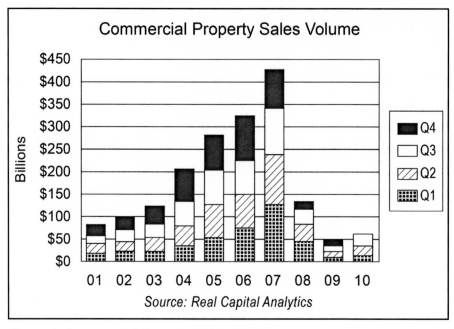

Figure 4: Commercial Property Sales Volume

CoStar Group, Inc., of Bethesda, Md., is renowned as the leading source of analytics and news publications in the commercial real estate sector. Its report, "Risky CRE Lending Deadly for Banks," published on February 17, 2010, may very well be one of the best market indicators with respect to the challenge and thus the opportunity, as summarized by the following excerpt and commentary:

> "Federal Reserve examiners are reporting a sharp deterioration in the credit performance of loans in banks' portfolios and loans in commercial mortgage-backed securities (CMBS)," Jon D. Greenlee, associate director, Division of Banking Supervision and Regulation for the Federal Reserve Board, told the Congressional Oversight Panel at a Field Hearing in January. "Of the approximately $3.5 trillion of outstanding debt associated with CRE, including loans for multifamily housing developments, about $1.7 trillion was held on the books of banks and thrifts, and an additional $900 billion represented collateral for CMBS, with other investors holding the remaining balance of $900 billion."

"Of note, more than $500 billion of CRE loans will mature each year over the next few years," Greenlee continued in his testimony. "In addition to losses caused by declining property cash flows and deteriorating conditions for construction loans, losses will also be boosted by the depreciating collateral value underlying those maturing loans. These losses will place continued pressure on banks' earnings, especially those of smaller regional and community banks that have high concentrations of CRE loans."

"Over the next few years, a wave of commercial real estate loan failures could threaten America's already-weakened financial system. The Congressional Oversight Panel is deeply concerned that commercial loan losses could jeopardize the stability of many banks, particularly the nation's mid-size and smaller banks, and that as the damage spreads beyond individual banks that it will contribute to prolonged weakness throughout the economy," the report concluded.

Between 2010 and 2014, about $1.4 trillion in commercial real estate loans are expected to reach the end of their terms. By Congressional Oversight Panel estimates, nearly $700 billion of that debt is presently "underwater," a situation in which the borrower owes more than the current value of the underlying property. "It is difficult to predict either the number of foreclosures to come or who will be most immediately affected," the report concluded. "In the worst-case scenario, hundreds more community and mid-sized banks could face insolvency. Because these banks play a critical role in financing the small businesses that could help the American economy create new jobs, their widespread failure could disrupt local communities, undermine the economic recovery, and extend an already painful recession."

The problems facing commercial real estate have no single cause, according to the Congressional Oversight Panel. The loans they identified as most likely to fail were made at the height of the real estate bubble when commercial real estate values had been driven above sustainable levels and loans. The panel also noted that many loans were made carelessly in a rush for profit.

Federal Deposit Insurance Corporation (FDIC) insures depositors (not bank shareholders) and provides oversight to "insure" a bank's liquidity and viability. Many have felt that the FDIC Watch List should be something more visible to the general public. The FDIC does not publish its list of banks or the thrift institutions on its ailing list—otherwise known as the FDIC Bank Watch List. However, private companies do publish ratings on banks. The FDIC has compiled a list of these private ratings services, which is available on the Internet and through third parties such as DebtX and First Financial, which have contracts for managing dissemination of certain offerings to qualified buyers.[1]

The FDIC does explicitly state that this list of private ratings firms is in no way an endorsement by the FDIC. Basically, there is no guarantee that these private firms' data about banks reflects the FDIC data, but it's probably a safe bet that they're close.

By regulation, the banks must adjust the value of their assets to the market value. This ensures the asset value (and net equity) is of current value and not inflated. The bank regulator must balance the two social goals of limiting risk in the banking system while allowing for the production of the desired level of loans and deposits. This can be difficult because in limiting risk, the regulator cannot force private agents to abide by bank regulations because private agents can always choose not to participate as equity holders in banks. In other words, regulations that make the cost of capital in banking too high will result in a banking system that is too small; regulations that are too lax result in a larger banking system, but possibly one that is too risky.

Many banks have been able to push out of the erosion of their exposure due in part to TARP (Troubled Asset Relief Program). TARP is a program by the United States government to purchase assets and equity from financial institutions to strengthen its financial sector. It was signed into law by President George W. Bush on October 3, 2008, and was a component of the government's measures in 2008 to address the subprime mortgage crisis.

TARP allows the United States Department of the Treasury to purchase or insure up to $700 billion of "troubled assets," defined as:

> (A) residential or commercial mortgages and any securities, obligations, or other instruments that are based on or related to such mortgages, that in each case was originated or issued on or before March 14, 2008, the purchase of which the Secretary determines promotes financial market stability; and (B) any other financial instrument that the Secretary, after consultation with the Chairman of the Board of Governors of the Federal Reserve System, determines the purchase of which is necessary to promote financial market stability, but only upon transmittal of such determination, in writing, to the appropriate committees of Congress.[2]

In short, TARP allows the Treasury to purchase illiquid, difficult-to-value assets from banks and other financial institutions. The targeted assets can be collateralized debt obligations, which were sold in a booming market until 2007, when they were hit by widespread foreclosures on the underlying loans. TARP was to improve the liquidity of these assets by purchasing them using secondary market mechanisms, thus allowing participating institutions to stabilize their balance sheets and avoid further losses. TARP does not allow banks to recoup losses already incurred on troubled assets, but officials expect that once trading of these assets resumes, their prices will stabilize and ultimately increase in value, resulting in gains to both participating banks and the Treasury itself. The concept of future gains from troubled assets comes from the hypothesis in the financial industry that these assets are oversold, as only a small percentage of all mortgages are in default, while the relative fall in prices represents losses from a much higher default rate. A major portion of TARP, in exchange for warrants to stock, was issued whereby, as part of the equity (capital infusion), the government would have a stock position—a form of guarantee by the bank to make sure it was not without consideration.

The published list of banks and other financial institutions covered by TARP include:

Citigroup

Bank of America

JP Morgan Chase

Wells Fargo

GMAC Financial Services

General Motors

Goldman Sachs

Morgan Stanley

PNC Financial Services Group

U.S. Bankcorp

Chrysler

Capital One Financial

Reions Financial Corporation

American Express

Bank of New York Mellon Corp.

State Street Corporation

Discover Financial

As a matter of record, the FDIC is responsible for insuring depositor funds to the disclosed limits and therefore monitoring the bank's operations and financial condition. Banks borrow funds with leverage from the Federal Reserve. The Federal Reserve is the central bank of the United States. Its unique structure includes a federal government agency, the Board of Governors, in Washington, D.C., and 12 regional reserve banks.

There were a lot of fortunes made as a result of structure that shifted and adjusted values during the RTC days. Many feel that the financial crunch and economic challenge of today is a result of loose lending practices in the residential industry, the explosion of CMBS (Commercial Mortgage Backed Securities), world unrest, and of course, increase in unemployment.

For the remainder of this chapter, we will focus on how the banks are dealing with diminishing asset values and their crippling effect on their balance sheet and growth of distressed assets, which—for the opportunity investor—is the target in discount prices.

Before we get too deep in the valuation of the asset, let's take a brief look at what goes on from the bank side of the business. Remember, a loan is a liability to the borrower, but an asset to the bank. There will be a test at the end of this chapter (just kidding, but important to remember).

How to Find Non-Performing Loans and REO Properties

The goal is to target the banks with high Texas Ratios. The Texas Ratio was developed as an early warning system to identify potential problem banks. It was developed by Gerard Cassidy and others at RBC Capital Markets, and it is calculated by dividing the value of the lender's non-performing assets (non-performing loans + real estate owned) by the sum of its tangible common equity capital and loan loss reserves. RBC Capital Markets is part of a leading provider of financial services, Royal Bank of Canada (RBC). Operating since 1869, RBC has more than $721 billion in assets and one of the highest credit ratings of any financial institution, according to Moody's AA1 and Standard & Poor's AA-. RBC is one of the strongest, most stable banks globally and has a Tier 1 Capital Ratio of 13.2 percent. By market capitalization, RBC is among the top 20 largest banks globally and is the 6th largest in North America.

Here's the formula for calculating the Texas Ratio:

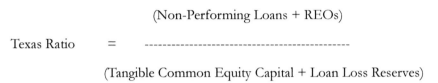

$$\text{Texas Ratio} = \frac{\text{(Non-Performing Loans + REOs)}}{\text{(Tangible Common Equity Capital + Loan Loss Reserves)}}$$

Cassidy noted that, in analyzing Texas banks during the early 1980s recession, banks tended to fail when this ratio reached 1:1, or 100 percent. During the 1990s recession (ibid RTC), he noted a similar pattern among New England banks. Banks are sized in terms of assets, (e.g., $100 million community bank, $1 billion regional bank, or $150+ billion—such as Wells Fargo, which has national presence).

Tables of high Texas Ratio banks are probably the next best substitute for the actual unpublished FDIC Bank Watch List. The updated tables can be viewed by going to: Amateur-Investor.net/TexasRatio.htm

Although Texas Ratio is quite useful in helping to identify weak banks that need more scrutiny, it can't predict which bank will fail next. It is not a perfect indicator. The data from the FDIC is always several months old. Some banks may improve by raising additional capital or merging with another bank. Currently, additional capitalization from TARP is not accurately reflected. Conversely, some larger banks may be in far worse condition than Texas Ratio indicates, since certain exotic troubled assets such as collateralized debt obligations and mortgage-backed securities are not reflected.

Amateur-Investor.net (Amateur-Investor.net/TexasRatio.htm) provides online analytics and updates to the banking watch list and utilizes the Texas Ratio as a modeling and watch factor tool. Also, there are a number of factors that can cause a bank to have a high Texas Ratio, so a bank with a high Ratio will not necessarily fail.[3]

As of the fourth quarter of 2010, 375 banks had a Texas Ratio of 100 or above, while 651 banks had a Texas Ratio between 50 and 99. Keep in mind that there are around 7,666 banks in the U.S., so that means only 5 percent have a Texas Ratio above 100. Comparing Texas Ratio Data sources, one can obtain a list of the High Texas Ratio banks for any state via Google by going to DepositAccounts.com.

Another valuable resource that provides an updated index of industry metrics is Banktracker: MSNBC.MSN.com/banks.[4] There are other analytics, such as the Troubled Asset Ratio Indicator, which is an interesting source for comparison of Texas Ratio-like indicators. It correlates well with Texas Ratio, is accurate, the methodology is well explained, and it is a very handy cross-check for data.

Reserves

Sizing the bank may have an impact on the level of reserves. Many feel the life of the community bank (i.e., under $100 million in assets) or even one under the $1 billion bracket is on the brink of extinction, much like GM eliminating Oldsmobile and Pontiac. Such is the course of history in that big banks have already begun the process (e.g., Wells Fargo's consolidation with Wachovia, Bank of America acquiring the assets of Countrywide, or the Chase acquisition of Washington Mutual).

The FDIC has legacy loans or non-performing loans (NPL) that were obtained from the banks it had to close. Discounts are based on discounts "to," not discounts "of"—what I refer to in this book as "cents on the dollar." They'll sell these assets at deep discounts, such as 50 to 60 percent, to very qualified buyers. We know of pools that may be even less, such as FDIC-sponsored, JV (joint venture), or loss share that could be as low as 30 percent.

Loss share is a program by which the acquisition bank partners with the FDIC, and the FDIC covers 80 percent of the loss. Normally, the FDIC sells bulk portfolios from $100 million, and it will finance up to 90 percent of the purchase. For example, One West Bank (California), which took over IndyMac Bank (also California) has bought legacy loans from the FDIC using this FDIC REO and NPL financing program. (See FDIC.gov for disclosure and programs.) Also, Fannie Mae and Freddie Mac offer similar REO and NPL programs. Hedge funds are major players in this private market. They break up the $100 million portfolios into $5 million to $25 million portfolios and resell them at 65 to 80 percent on the dollar to smaller, more agile buyers.

Yury Iofe of Universal Business Structured Solutions states that his company will finance up to 70 percent of an REO and NPL bulk portfolio's purchase price.

Thus, the buyer can leverage 70 percent and only have to invest 30 percent of their own money.[5]

In many cases, the bank REO and NPL seller will finance the purchase with a new bank loan to the buyer. The maximum LTV tends to be 70 percent. The interest rate and terms of the new loan are very attractive: prime rate (WJS, Federal Discount Rate, 11th District Cost of Funds) + 1 percent, with a small amount of closing costs. They may offer a "price discount" of 15 to 25 percent, depending on their FDIC Texas Ratio. Banks with a Texas Ratio of 100 percent are prime targets for REO and NPL bulk sales.

I collaborate with many experts who have either consulted with or come from the banking industry. One of our close affiliates, Randy Long from Atlanta, has over 15 years of experience from the bank side of the business and offers the following strategies for working with banks:

1. Target asset managers.

Target the asset managers of high Texas Ratio banks to obtain direct off-market REO and NPL bulk portfolios. Typically, the banks will sell for 65 percent or more if it's a bulk sale, i.e., $10+ million. There are 12 California banks that have Texas Ratios exceeding 100 percent. Also, there are private equity firms (PEF) that will pay up to 70 percent for SFR and up to 60 percent for commercial real estate. These PEFs are very sound financially and are direct buyers. The larger the portfolio, the better and more likely they will be to discuss a sell-off. It's a matter of economy of scale.

Kondaur Capital (California notes), Conix Capital (Arizona), and ClearVue Capital (California) are viewed as some of the big players. They issue a formal letter of intent (LOI) within 5 to 7 days after receiving an REO or NPL tape and only need 20 days for due diligence, and then 10 days to close. Oftentimes, they use a 30- to 60-day quick-sell strategy for the takedown and an REO or NPL value as the price they will pay. They raise capital from wealthy individuals through opportunity funds. Then they market and sell the properties individually.

The higher the price point to par (i.e., book value), the more likely a transaction will result. Price points vary from market to market, asset to asset, and bank to bank. Seventy cents on the dollar or 70 percent to book may be a gift to one bank and not enough to a bank that is financially stronger and could hold out for 75 to 80 percent. Buyers usually provide their BPO (broker price opinion) appraisals to the seller or banks to help convince the banks that their value is the correct market value. Most fail to close because the bank can't take the hit to their balance sheets, which causes a higher Texas Ratio, or their board simply will not approve the large discount and will continue to try to sell the REOs individually. One can develop a lot of REO and NPL bank business, but may have little patience with the bulk buyers.

2. Begin with the bid process.

As a rule of thumb, banks are required to limit their exposure to 25 percent for one individual borrowing source and/or a certain dollar amount determined by either their federal regulators, OTS (Office of Thrift Supervision), OCC (Office of the Comptroller of the Currency), or other regulating bodies. One strategy is to draft the LOI subject to due diligence and include a worksheet as an exhibit.

To create the worksheet, upload the seller's Excel spreadsheet, delete properties you don't want to bid on, create another column next to the seller's list price or UPB (unpaid balance) for your bid per property and another column bid price or a percent per property, then total down the three columns. Use initial LOI templates and fill in the blank forms. Most of the bulk portfolio OREO/REO/NPL industry follows this format and initial bid process, sometimes referred to as an indicative bid.

In bid situations, the subject more often will be sufficient to show your intent without obligation until accepted. Be prepared to offer a good faith negotiated deposit of up to 10 percent included in the initial LOI. Then, don't do anything further on that portfolio until you have an accepted, signed, and returned the initial LOI from the portfolio seller.

3. Know your bid price percentages for different property types.

Pre-set individual bid price percentages for each property type. Thirty percent for land, 40 percent for lots, 60 percent for commercial real estate, 70 percent for a 2-4 family, 75 percent for SFR, and 85 percent for multi-family apartments, OREO, and REO are just some of the general price points by asset class. Bid percentages may be 10 to 20 percent—plus or minus, depending on area, condition, quality, age, occupancy, and a number of other factors of the asset. This is what makes dealing with commercial properties more of an art than a science. In this regard, residential bids are fairly easy in that by local MLS (Multiple Listing Service), comparables make the residential an apples-to-apples market or relative price comparison.

Once you know your bid price percentages, do an initial interview with the seller and start your due diligence, which should take 15 to 30 days for normal-size portfolios. Then, issue your final bid. Once accepted, set up the escrow closing, wire transfer of funds, performance of terms and conditions, etc. At that point, you'll be competitive in the industry.

Few initial LOIs are accepted by banks. Calculate your final bid price from current FMV (fair market value) or BPO. Most institutional distressed asset and note PEFs use a realtor's current BPO, which costs between $75 and $100. Don't forget to include a property's site inspection, site sketch, pictures (street view, front view, rear view, interior upgrades, and repairs required), three to four sold comps within 1 mile and six months' time including any repos, two to three current listings, property write-up, and opinion.

4. **Develop contacts in the banks.**

When working the REO market full-time, call 30 to 40 banks per day. Request to speak to the special asset/OREO VP or manager. For banks and financial institutions, request to speak to the commercial and business development or lending officer (for loan referrals) and the special asset manager for REOs and NPLs. Remember, they get dozens of calls a day, so have a script ready to deliver a succinct and consistent message. Have a natural and compelling presentation that motivates them to take the call and listen to you. Keep it short and to the point. You may reach only *one* asset manager and have to leave messages for the others.

Try to obtain the specific asset VP or manager's contact info, including email address, before or just after leaving a message. Then, use their email address to solicit them at least two times per month. Over a period of time, you will have created a business relationship and a brand name for REO and NPLs. Most individuals call once and that's it; however, if a person pursues banks with $900+ million in assets and a Texas Ratio between 60 and 200 percent, then ideally the target bank should have $1+ billion and Texas Ratios of 50 to 130 percent, as these tend to have the most interest.

Call back the target banks up to seven times over a 1- to 1.5-month period, relentlessly. Persistence will pay off. I mentioned above to have a script ready and to practice it to ensure you have a smooth delivery. Your script should be a brief verbal elevator presentation: selling the features, benefits, and advantages of your plan and execution. Do not fabricate anything. Ask for the business and to be included on their distribution of tapes, or other non-performing, hard-to-move assets or notes. The asset managers who are interested in your service will send the bank's confidentiality agreement (CA) to you for ratification. Return it promptly, and you'll start receiving their REO and NPL Excel tapes and other inventory. The rest of the REO and NPL process starts from there: this is the beginning of a relationship.

5. **Be patient and persistent.**

Typically, multiple bids may produce an initial acceptance of *one* LOI. The banks have become quite familiar with the process: expectations, buyer performance (or lack of), and customer service. Some have never sold bulk, just individual properties, so the 50+ acceptances may only lead to one closing. That's the way it works! If a person closes four bulk sales a year, they're lucky. Most of the initial closing may be just a few properties and not the majority of the bulk. Thus, there's a huge difference between your potential income and your actual income. If you keep marketing yourself and/or your company, over time you create a large lead databank. Stay focused, and keep repeating the process; this is what works on a consistent basis with asset managers. In most cases, you'll only reach 2-3 people per day and leave messages for the rest. There's a lot of work involved; however, there's also much satisfaction with large rewards from relentless effort. Remember, most will give up on the first one or two calls, so persistence will pay off. You will need to have a system that is consistent—one that can be tracked and measured.

Inventory on the Horizon

Shadow inventory is REO and NPL inventory that has not been listed or pooled, and therefore not released. Shadow inventory can be made up of both commercial and residential real estate properties that were held up from bank REOs by moratoriums that have recently expired. The shadow inventory for CRE is $1.5 trillion, and the shadow inventory for residential is $2.6 trillion! Thus, the banks will have plenty of NPLs and REOs to sell, and so will the lending agencies (FNMAE, FHLMC, GNMA, USDA, FHA, VA), regulators FDIC and FHLBB, prime and non-prime mortgage bankers, credit unions, life insurance companies (CRE), and commercial finance companies (GE Capital). So far, the lending agencies, wholesale mortgage lenders, and the CRE credit companies are the big sellers.

Retail and Secondary Market

Retail is known as the primary market, and wholesale is known as the secondary market. Lending correspondents (who use warehouse lines to fund loans) and brokers (whose loans are table-funded by lenders) are approved licensees by the wholesale lender/investors, governments, and/or regulators to represent the wholesale lender as a distributor—sometimes exclusively—of their product or service to the primary market. Primary market transactions referral-source the networks that refer their transactions to secondary market investors. Likewise, markets that deal with REO and NPL create the primary and secondary portals.

It is imperative that the conversation is pertinent to the audience. Think of it this way: retail is the end user and wholesale is the pass-through or investor market. Wholesale mortgage lending consists of buying groups of mortgages from primary market lenders (e.g., banks, credit unions, mortgage companies, and apartment lenders) and selling them to secondary market investors such as Fannie Mae, Freddie Mac, Ginnie Mae, Wall Street investment bank conduits, private equity funds, hedge funds, and REITs. What does this all mean? There are a myriad of sellers that have equally as many strategies and challenges, and thus the opportunity investor is not tied down to one specific provider to shop for the asset type, asset disposition, or opportunity to acquire a distressed asset.

The Major Real Estate Companies

The major real estate companies have been buyers of bulk REO for some time now. Companies like Coldwell Banker (California), Weichert Realtors (Northeast Group), and CB Richard Ellis (CRE) have all been positioning to profit not only from their sales commissions, but also from the difference between the portfolio›s wholesale purchase price and the eventual retail sales price. In many cases, because of their branding, public stock strength, institutional and political insight, and other highly visible factors, they are able to purchase at 10 to 30 percent on 100-million to 1-billion-size pools. Buying larger than $100 million portfolios may earn them from 13 to 46 percent or more, depending on whether it is both their listing and their sale.

Small real estate brokerages may use a securities company (e.g., UBS LOC) to leverage and purchase the REO assets, or they may use a small business or bank loan. Most real estate brokerages may be buyer prospects for REOs in that it gets them traction in today's investor sights while providing a cash flow of commissions. Cash, hedge, and equity funds, family trusts, and the like are good targets for buyers seeking transactional opportunities.

Summary of Chapter:

Like any industry of completion, it is always better to have an understanding of how the industry works from the ground up. It's like having an inside track. Use bank terminology, empathy, and dialogue that speaks to their challenges. You can't imagine how many of your competitors have no idea what they're doing and rush in with ridiculous offers, claims, and tactics to try to force the banks to listen. It will not work. Having backup statistics, knowledge of Texas Ratio, and a strategy to help reposition distressed and toxic assets makes you an ally—not an adversary.

References:

1. Federal Deposit Insurance Corporation (FDIC) Site: FDIC.gov.

2. Wikipedia: en.Wikipedia.org/wiki/Troubled_Asset_Relief_Program#cite_note-cbo.gov-7.

3. Amateur-Investor.net: Amateur-Investor.net/TexasRatio.htm.

4. MSNBC Investigative Reporting Workshop: Banktracker.MSNBC.MSN.com/banks.

5. Universal Business Structured Solution; 10 Shalks Rd., Princeton, NJ 08540; 888-778-1434; Y. Iofe, personal communication, March 15, 2011.

Prior to calculating the final bid, run MyNeighorhood.com or other computer CMA (comparative market analysis) for a quick ballpark price range of the neighborhood. A lot of these are free or have a small monthly fee. Think of bids as advertising and a measure of your customer service. The quicker you issue the LOI and the more professional and competitive you appear, the more banks will use and recommend you. Try to find out the types of properties, their locations, their condition, and what the bank will accept prior to requesting or accepting REO and NPL pools or tapes. If the bank is unrealistic, you don't want the properties. This will save everyone a lot of time. Regardless, put them on an REO or NPL Outlook email marketing or contact databank and send the bank monthly solicitations to keep your name in the queue. Eventually, some will finally decide to sell. One may have to solicit one bank 10 times before they send a tape. The more professional you are when they decide to sell, the more likely you are to be contacted. Over time, you will build up a large referral base.

"When it's obvious that a goal cannot be reached, don't adjust the goal, adjust the action steps." —*Chinese proverb*

CHAPTER NINE

What Works, What Doesn't

Over the past several years, I have kept an informal journal of what seems to work and what doesn't. It's like the adage, "It's what you don't know that will hurt the most." So this chapter will save you years and maybe hundreds of thousands of dollars. You can minimize false starts and schemes that will suck you in if you're aware of the telltale signs.

Vetting

Now, I have to admit I used the word "vetting" with intention and results long before I knew its origin, but found it interesting to discover how it came about and how it is now used in the financial community. Wikipedia gives us this definition:

> To *vet* was originally a horse-racing term, referring to the requirement that a horse be checked for health and soundness by a veterinarian before being allowed to race. Thus, it has taken the general meaning "to check."
>
> It is a figurative contraction of *veterinarian*, which originated in the mid-17th century. The colloquial abbreviation dates to the 1860s; the verb form of the word, meaning "to treat an animal," came a few decades later—according to the *Oxford English Dictionary*, the earliest known usage is 1891—and was applied primarily in a horse-racing context (e.g., "He vetted the stallion before the race," "You should vet that horse before he races."). By the early 1900s, *vet* had begun to be used as a synonym for *evaluate*, especially in the context of searching for flaws.[1]

So, with that context, we move to vetting's association and how to make best use of the intent and benefits for notes and deeds. First, I am always suspicious when there is no phone number or signature block of a company on an offer that can be checked out, and the anonymity of the offer itself. Use common sense! Someone who claims they have direct control, are the seller mandate or attorney for the lender, and have another ten authority claims should be able to provide evidence. Ask for a Letter of Authority (LOA), which will provide such credibility. Be cautious of the use of "seller's attorney" or "seller mandate," as these are usually red flags indicating that there is no LOA and that the writer is using the offer as an invitation to use the buyer's funds or credit to shop for product.

The second alarm, which is more commonly used, is a blind letter of intent (LOI) and proof of funds (POF). The word "blind," in this case, refers to an unknown product, value, specifics, condition, ownership, and sometimes even location. Now, I'm sure I could come up with some sarcastic analogies such as, "I have a car for sale, but before I tell you about it, you must make a deposit. Trust me; it's exactly what you want." You can surmise how foolish this sounds, yet we see this every day in offers, emails, phone calls, and webinars. Along these same lines are demands for POF, deposits into attorney trust accounts, total balance to escrow, and other loss of control for the buyer funds.

Here's the protocol we find most acceptable among vetted buyers and sellers. First, a sanitized sample of the product is provided as evidence of the pool, tape, or asset. Upon that verification, a LOI is written with a POF, and a contract is written. In my experience, any request for a blind LOI and POF is just an invitation to have the funds shopped to fulfill, or worse, used as POF for someone else's private agenda.

Gross-Up

This happens when there are multiple touch points in the path of a direct seller and direct buyer. What usually happens is that each touch point will add a point (i.e., 1 percent), and thus it is easy to determine how many people stand in the way of the deal going down. Believe it or not, some will mark it up more than 1 point, so if you hear "$100 million plus 4 points," you know it is a waste of time to get access to the selling source. We've actually been approached with a 6-point gross-up who swore they were direct, and of course we dismissed their promises and suggestions.

Pool and Share

Pool and share is a technique in which the daisy chain parties know that their contribution is just a name and number, suggest the transaction would never happen without their contribution, and therefore conclude that all the parties should split the fee equally. Again, at the end of the day, one person will do all the work. The person most direct to the seller will most likely have to package, vet the product, manage the paperwork, vet the buying parties, and dismiss those who stand in the way of a direct buy/sell transaction. Pool and share is also a sign that there are obstacles in the direct path of the buy/sell process, and it is highly unlikely the transaction will consummate.

Hedge and Equity Funds

Suppose the fund needs to obtain an 18 percent annual return, and the fund mission is to turn the product four times a year (every 120 days). That means they expect to make 4.5 percent on each flip. If the fee is 3 percent on each transaction, then that means the broker would be making 66.66 percent of the equivalent profit on a transaction for which they put up the money. That is why the hedge and equity funds will only pay 1 percent, if that. The other reason they will not pay more than 1 percent is because having multiple brokers involved, they shouldn't have to pay more than one person, and thus .5 to 1 percent should be more than enough for the direct source.

Billion-Dollar Deals

There are no "billion-dollar" pools in the streets. These are highly regulated transactions done between "good old boys" on Wall Street or at the institutional level. We, as a practice, blacklist anyone claiming to be direct to billion-dollar activities. These deals are done on fractions of basis points between traders and Wall Street firms over cocktails at lunch without ever being floated around, or else they are marketed in the streets by brokers, intermediaries, or even worse, "mandates."

Fees

At the time of this writing, 65 cents on the dollar in California as a blended pool is near retail. In California, whether it's Orange County (OC) or the Bay Area or another major MSA market, product priced at $200,000 to 400,000 with no rehab might work. Blended California is in the 60 range in that Barstow, Stockton, and

Fresno are 56 range, and OC is in the 64 to 65 range, so 65 cents on the dollar blended is a retail offering.

Here's the other reason why it's a retail offering. Those buying SFR for resale are looking at 85 percent to the comparable market value to resell faster than the short sales in the same area. At 85 cents to the comp or BPO, that means they have to load the deal with 5 percent fees, 1 percent closing cost, and 10 percent minimum profit—that's at least 17 percent. 85-17=68! That means at 65 + 3 points, they are at a break-even with no surprises. That is the number-one reason a fee of 3 points on $100 million is a flag: the 3-point fee could be more than what the investor's profit would be at the end, and the investor still needs to do all the work, take the risk, and get a return on capital. No one will pay 3 points on $100 million, let alone on $500 million. That would be $15 MILLION!

Do the math, and know what your real buyers will pay and the price points. Again, I have found that a declining-tier Lehman schedule is generally accepted as a standard for fees.

1 percent on $100 million is $1million.

2 percent on $100 million is $2 million.

3 percent on $100 million is $3 million.

The point is, if the buyer is going to make a percent of profit from the transaction, their entire net after expense profit may only be 5 to 10 percent, in which case paying out 3 percent could be more than 50 percent of their entire transaction profit. Therefore, any transaction of 3 percent on $100 million is inflated beyond a generally acceptable margin.

Create a Database of Closely Held Subscribers

Create a direct-seller and direct-buyer database-to-email prospect list in ACT, CRM, or Outlook. Email newsletter flyers monthly and status updates weekly. There are times you cannot compete on price; however, you can always compete on customer service and providing personal attention to detail!

Other avenues for building a database include becoming an active member of many real estate and financial institution associations. Join, network, volunteer, be a public speaker, trainer, or sponsor. Collect business cards, enter them into your contact databank, and solicit them.

Set Your Expectations and Goals

One may close just four to six transactions a year in institutional sales, but earn a lot more money than the masses do—in less time, with fewer costs and hassles than "the somewhat retail market." For example, suppose your average closing is a $5 million portfolio, six times a year, times a 1.5 percent fee, equaling $450,000.00. With very little cost and time involved, $5 million is considered a small portfolio. As our strategy partner, now a retired banker, states, "Just one of the portfolios closed at $45 million from one bank to one private equity fund within three months of the date of my solicitation to closing and dispersal of escrow funding." That's hard to beat.

How to Raise Funds

Consider raising capital for an opportunity fund from angel investors, wealth funds, venture capitalists, stockbrokers, REIs, and small hedge funds. Then, pursue buying the bank portfolios and selling the individual properties—and very small bulks—to mid-large real estate companies (e.g., Coldwell Banker, CB Richard Ellis), wealthy individuals, and small groups of vetted buyers, among others. Sell larger pools to the Private Equity Funds (PEFs) and Private Investment Trusts (PITs) Silicon Valley has the greatest concentration of angel and venture funds in the world—a great source to tap!

Buy the Bank, the Assets of the Bank, or Both

There is an increasing drive to purchase assets from troubled banks, or in some cases, to purchase the bank and shore up the balance sheet with added capital. Negotiating to purchase the bank would help the bank solve a problem. Meet with the bank ownership to discuss what the bank needs to succeed, whether it's to dispose of assets, infuse money, clean up a balance sheet, or dispose of the bank. This possibility creates an opportunity for a bank to survive an FDIC takeover threat or other major setbacks, to simplify a complex situation and address the issues.

Summary of Chapter:

The purpose of this chapter is to expand on actions and processes that work and to highlight those that waste a great deal of time and money. Most of the situations reflect commonsense awareness; however, due to anxiety and greed, it may become easy to ignore the obvious. Cash is king, so deal from a position of strength, and protect the buyer's interest. There are a myriad of scams with the intent to gross-up fees, obtain use of a buyer's funds for personal benefit, or create an atmosphere of product and want. Adhere to prudent business practices, use third-party verification, and above all, be sure only to deal with direct or vetted sources that have the seller's LOA.

References:

1. Wikipedia: en.Wikipedia.org/wiki/Vetting.

CHAPTER TEN

How to Balance
Risk and Reward

We touched on this earlier with regard to the SFR and REO market: there is a strike price that is commensurate with a risk/reward valuation. In Chapter Seven, we used the scenario of acquisition of a single or small pool of California SFR at 65 cents with the intent to resell at 85 cents, and thus be below the comparable in the market for a fast turn. In this example, the cost of acquisition, spread, cost to hold, taxes, insurance, rehab, and profit were all included with the result of 10 percent profit for a 90-day hold, or 40 percent annual profit.

Residential real estate is certainly easier in that the comparables are easy to get on Zillow or MLS. Also, there is still funding via FHA and conventional lenders. The price points are smaller and an investor can easily select a market, geography, or sweet spot to their liking. If the property doesn't sell in the course of the flip strategy, the property can always be rented, leased, optioned, or offered as a sale with seller financing, thus cushioning any loss of capital. Last, regarding risk/reward with residential, is the fact that the price points are smaller, so if there is a loss for miscalculation, the amount is most likely less than a comparable commercial property.

My experience is that the more experienced the investor, the more likely they are to use third-party resources: contractors, management, outside contractors, and tax and legal advisors. It's difficult to do everything yourself, so delegation is a critical strategy to executing a successful plan. There are occasions and situations where having employees and a staff for full- and part-time services, maintenances, operations, even accounting is more cost effective. The thread here is to use experts to minimize guessing and thus reduce some of the risk factors.

We often hear that successful investors are quick to make decisions and slow to make change. Experience plays a big factor in making quick decisions, so having a plan, a checklist, due diligence, and acquisition and exit strategies may help to improve the reward and minimize the risk.

Art vs. Science

Risk/reward is a combination of art and science. There are factors that can be measured to the penny and others that are variables based on events yet to happen. The stronger the evidence on the science side, the less likely the art will interfere with the end result or objective.

Many industries—medical, sales, marketing, education, entertainment—have both an art and a science to the problem or objective. History often plays a defining role in how one can convert the art to the science. The art aspect is the reasoning, motivation, emotion, interpretation, personal value, timing, hold period, and a number of other subjective reasons. Why do you think it takes 8 to 10 years to get a medical degree? One reason is because the likelihood of converting the art to science mitigates error, and in life-and-death situations, you would like to know those in charge have mastered the science more than the art.

For our discussion of real estate, the science aspect incorporates the hard facts, physical condition, historical financial situation, due diligence, acquisition strategy, exit strategy, management, operations, calculation of financial benefits (e.g., ROI, IRR, cash-on-cash), and other factors that can be measured.

On the other hand, commercial real estate tends to have more variables, and therefore may be more risky for a number of reasons, including:

1. market absorption

2. condition and cost of rehab or tenant improvements

3. code compliance

4. fewer banks lending on commercial assets

5. higher cost of funding

6. more equity required

7. shorter terms for debt structure

8. quality of tenant

9. acquisition and exit strategies

10. investor tolerance

11. duration of hold

The following sections may provide some insight and variables in analyzing risk/reward.

Tolerance

I like to compare active vs. passive investors, i.e., are you comfortable in hiring someone to manage your investment (passive), or is your threshold more hands-on (active)? An active investment with an owner-operator business model is like a 20-room motel vs. a 200-room, flagged, full-service hotel where professional management may be the better choice due to factors such as the size, employees, cost to maintain, restaurant, bar, retail, parking, and pool/spa. You get the picture. If you can afford third-party services on the 20-room motel, it's like having management on a duplex.

Every investment has risk, even bond-rated investments with Credit A tenants and triple-net leases. Other than a government-guaranteed 30-, 40-, or 50-year U.S. Post Office with a 4 percent coupon, all tenants (even credit tenants) have some level of risk (e.g., Circuit City, Borders, Hollywood Video, and other formerly successful tenants who have gone out of business).

Patience

Another factor to assess is your level of patience. Everyone is familiar with the term "turns" as it relates to the movement of inventory. Grocery stores are a familiar snapshot of high turn, low margin. Consider how many times the milk rack is filled in the course of a given day. POS systems can now track to the minute and provide automated fulfillment all the way back to the purchasing, supplier, distribution center, logistic management, marketing, price management, and other online communications.

Fast flips may not be this automated, but the message is that fast turns require less demand on margin, and therefore the annualized margin can be significant. Assume that a moderate 10 percent margin on a residential flip every 90 days will add up to a 40 percent annualized margin. A number of risk factors could affect a fast-moving strategy in that a holding for more than 90 days or a margin below 10 percent could affect the net result. Also, since the residential market can move in 30-day swings, the risk has a different weight than the reward.

On the other hand, fast flips may not meet the needs of a three-to-five-year hold strategy for more conservative investors. Commercial transactions may include assignment, wholesale, holds and other factors.

Why is this important? Typically, the greater your patience level, the more likely your goals and expectations will be reached. The shorter the hold time, the more likely the variables will have a lesser impact on the overall expectation. An example could be this table of a 10-year hold and the expected IRR.

	Level w/o Appreciation		Unlevel w/o Appreciation		Level w/ 5% Appreciation	
Investment		(1,000,000)		(1,000,000)		(1,000,000)
Year 1	5%	50,000	4%	40,000	5%	50,000
Year 2	5%	50,000	6%	60,000	5%	50,000
Year 3	5%	50,000	5%	50,000	5%	50,000
Year 4	5%	50,000	5%	50,000	5%	50,000
Year 5	5%	50,000	5%	50,000	5%	50,000
Year 6	5%	50,000	5%	50,000	5%	50,000
Year 7	5%	50,000	5%	50,000	5%	50,000
Year 8	5%	50,000	5%	50,000	5%	50,000
Year 9	5%	50,000	5%	50,000	5%	50,000
Year 10	5%	1,000,000	5%	1,000,000	5%	1,100,000
Net IRR		4.59%		4.59%		5.39%
Difference				0.01%		0.80%

Table 3: Expected IRR

Think about it. If your plan was a 10-year, 5 percent, non-compounded, annualized return, what would be the effect if the first year yielded only 4 percent, and the next year 6 percent, compared to a straight-line 5 percent per year? From the table above, you will notice a .01 percent difference over the course of 10 years. The idea is that the longer the time (patience), the less likely minor infractions will affect the end results. Of course, situations will vary, so this is meant to be only a visual presentation of the concept. A 5 percent appreciation will have a much greater effect regarding the growth on capital (i.e., 5 percent will have a greater impact at the end than the annualized cash flow).

Many CRE professionals are students of the industry and have made a career out of it. Some have been in it for 10, 20, 30 years or more and have seen successful—and maybe some not so successful—years. If you think you can wake up one morning knowing everything, that's a disaster waiting to happen.

Cash Reserves

Cash reserves provide a cushion for the unknown. Most lenders know this and require a certain amount of reserves be set aside for repairs, vacancies, tenant improvements, and surprises. Frequently, the lender will cushion the amount that they will lend based on experience, oftentimes linked to asset type. This is why the income and expenses may be different when analyzed by the owner vs. the bank: the lender may load a reserve as an "anticipated" expense.

The lender will also use something called a debt service cover ratio or DSCR. This is a ratio based on a percentage of cushions the lender desires based on experience, industry, and competition in the debt market. For example, multifamily may be 1.10, which means there needs to be a 10 percent cushion between the NOI and the load to service the debt based on interest, terms, amortization, and other factors of the loan under consideration. Retail may have a DSCR of 1.30 based on the risk that losing one tenant could have a greater impact on the ability to meet the debt service obligation. The bottom line is that cash reserves are a cushion that could mitigate the risk.

Cash Flow

Cash flow can mitigate risk in that the properties have some level of performance. Assets that have cash flow (i.e., positive net income) are desired by investors who want a head start to their expected return. Most of the time, assets with cash flow will have fewer discounts for obvious reasons, e.g., there is a return on capital from the onset. Assets with cash flow, whether notes or deeds, may also be likely candidates for retail or listed offerings, and thus become more attractive to the masses.

Another factor that may work in favor of the lender's, seller's, or borrower's effort to modify or negotiate with assets that have cash flow is the appointment of a receiver. A receiver is an independent third party appointed by the court to oversee the asset for the benefit of the secured (and possibly the unsecured in the event of a petition for bankruptcy), thus ensuring the asset will be maintained and the income held in trust. This usually means that there is a timeline and strategy in place, although for the opportunity investor, it may actually work against deeper discounts in that there will be a history of income, stabilization, strategy to retail, and other factors increasing the value, which may have been the motivation of the opportunity investor or buyer. The good news is that, with a receiver, most assets that could otherwise go dormant, be vandalized, or be subject to other physical or economic obsolescence will not diminish in value.

An additional advantage to an appointed receiver is accessibility. As a neutral party, they are usually more engaged with the status and forthcoming with updates, due in part to the hands-on knowledge and timely requirements of reports to the lender and courts. We have found that an open, yet guarded, communication with receivers to keep abreast of the project or asset condition has helped to move the process forward faster when the timeline is established by the lender or court.

Value Add

"Value add" is the risk associated with assets that are not currently producing cash flow. Oftentimes, they are vacant, incomplete, fractured, environmentally affected, and require rehab, tenant improvements, or code repairs. The play is that there is more value in the end product than the existing asset. This also means there is more risk to the purchase, and usually the lender and seller are aware of the diminishing value, thus the discounts are deeper and more motivated.

Value add is not the same as appreciation, which is the normal course of increased value associated with time of hold, market trends, absorption, competition, and other factors of the asset increasing in value over time. Value add usually requires repositioning, modification to "highest and best use," additional capital infusion for tenant improvements, and other strategies to provide more value. Value add can also be associated with "upside" for some assets that may already have some cash flow, yet not maximized due to management, maintenance, updating, change-out of tenant mix, or other proactive efforts. A good example of value add is a retail center that replaces a façade, changes out doors and windows, brings in a national tenant, adds square footage, and acquires an adjacent parcel or assemblage. Repairing the weathered parking lot is not normally considered a value add, but would usually be classified as a maintenance or capital-reserve improvement.

A number of distressed assets will qualify as value add. A typical scenario might be a bank that has been taken over by the FDIC or other regulator who originated a construction loan for a borrower. In most cases, once the FDIC issues the cease and desist (C&D), the dedicated funds for the project are frozen since that bank is no longer in operation. This causes great hardship in that the project is stalled, and it's unlikely that rescue funds will be made available. The borrower would have to add his own new capital, find an investor to loan to finish, cash call if there is a partnership or other investor structure providing such, do a workout or modification, file a Chapter 11 for reorganization, or utilize another strategy to complete the project. Virtually all of these options are risky in that the cost to complete after a time of dormancy requires ramp-up, which could add costs beyond the hard dollars and cents. Therein lies the opportunity for a value add play.

1031

Many investors have some knowledge or experience with a 1031 exchange. Purchasing a distressed asset could be a high-reward strategy in the proverbial "sell high, buy low" strategy. Of course, always consult your tax and legal advisors in addition to 1031 qualified intermediaries (QIs), facilitators, and accommodators. There are some up-front risks in that the distressed asset may not be available to meet the timelines, or available at all due to agreements with the borrowers. It may also be pooled with other assets and sold without future notice or subject to other factors not normally associated with a single-seller asset.

With careful planning, both forward and reverse 1031 could be beneficial for a 1031 exchange. Remember, a 1031 is a "like kind" exchange, and for real estate it is usually deed for deed. A non-performing note in itself is not a qualified exchange; however, note after foreclose is fully qualified. The underlying deed of a non-performing note can be named—the technical term is "identified"—during the time of the exchange as long as the form of ownership is by title within the 180-day closing timeline. Purchase of a non-performing note is not "replacement of debt" and therefore cannot be used to qualify when seeking to cover the debt. Additional cash can always be infused to replace debt or to buy up in value.

Cap Rate

Capitalization rate (cap rate) is a benchmark tool used in financial analysis, and in terms of real estate is the relative rate of return. Virtually every discussion will begin with "What is the cap rate?" as a relative starting point. Think of it as, "What am I making on my investment?" thus the higher the return on the same investment, the more it reflects the price. The higher the cap rate, the lower the initial purchase price, and vice versa. The lower the cap rate, the higher the initial purchase price. So, opportunity investors in particular are looking for high cap rate: 9, 10, or 12 percent. Unfortunately, this also is an indication of risk in that the price is discounted for a reason—vacancy, obsolescence, distressed condition, or another reason. Generally, a low cap, i.e., 4, 5, or 7 percent, is based on a safety: high-valued property, trophy asset, credit or government tenant, or corporate guarantee.

Opportunity investors would like to have the safety of a 6 cap at the price of a 12 cap. The dilemma is that the two are at opposite ends of the spectrum, and the art of the deal is to find a middle ground that provides a suitable margin to engage. Most often, distressed assets do not have a cap rate since they are fractured, incomplete, vacant, underperforming, or require additional capital, and thus "distressed." If they are performing at an equivalent of a 10, 12, or 14 cap rate, then that would mean there is a net income based on value, and most likely they are not distressed. The balance in risk/reward is to determine whether a cap rate or value add strategy is driving the acquisition.

Cash-on-Cash

Cash-on-cash is another financial metric based on initial capital, leverage, additional capital requirement, and overall return on equity. The reason this is important to assess early on is to decide if leverage and debt is a good strategy for this particular asset. The cap rate described above is the return on capital assuming no leverage. The cash-on-cash (sometimes abbreviated as C/C) is inclusive of debt service, pre-pay penalties, or other costs of financial assistance.

The risks with leverage, of course, are the terms, the cash flow to service the obligation, the added oversight of a debt partner, encumbering the assets, and other risk associated with a mortgage or debt obligation.

IRR

Like a cap rate, internal rate of return (IRR) is a key financial metric to analyze acquisition-to-exit strategy. Cash flow is tracked not just on a net income basis, but is incorporated into the investment from start to finish. Excel and most financial calculators provide either a formula or calculator process that provides the entry of the acquisition, cash flow, tax benefits, and exit to be entered and based on the time of hold. This will yield an accurate IRR. The reason this is important when analyzing an asset, especially one that is distressed, is because it helps to set the expectation at the onset and also helps to uncover potential risk, requirements for cash infusion, hold period, exit target, return on capital, investor projection, and many other time-related and financial demands that would not be uncovered with due diligence.

It's not uncommon to run several IRR models based on acquisition, requirements for additional capital, expected changes in cash flow (if any), exit price points, time of hold or disposition, change in the debt model, or refinancing at a point of time.

Along with analyzing the NOI, ROI, cash flow, and cash-on-cash analysis, every acquisition should include an IRR, not only for the projection, but to model the expectation, help to minimize risk, and of course, to present an expectation of reward.

Hold Period

For those who foresaw the market downturn and sold in 2006 or early 2007, we wonder what insight they had or tools they used to assess the trouble on the horizon. Many, including the most sophisticated and knowledgeable experts with near-unlimited analysis resources, did not make the move soon enough or could not do it fast enough to unload or sell, and thus have taken the ride down with many players in the industry. The collapse of the CMBS and subprime and growing challenges in the banking industry are indeed timing issues.

In distressed assets, the hold period could be as short as an assignment, concurrent close, flip, short-term hold, or longer period based on a number of variables. The reason the asset is pigeonholed as distressed could be a result of evaporation of construction funds, takeout, matured funding, lack of capital to complete the repairs or build out, or simply the change in the economy and getting caught with the wrong asset at the wrong time.

When assessing risk/reward, it is crucial to determine the hold period and adhere to the strategy with a strong commitment and priority. For example, if the strategy is to flip within a year, then variables should be put in place to exit within that time frame. The reason for this is because the cost to hold or the return to the investor can be impacted by an extended hold more so than waiting for a market change to offset the added cost during the hold period. As they say, timing the market is never a good strategy.

Exit Strategy

One of the most powerful quotes and profound statements in the world of business is by the famous author Stephen Covey: "Begin with the end in mind." How true this is, and even more so in the distressed asset sector. As mentioned in other chapters and segments of this chapter, the exit has to be as important as—and in many cases the most important strategy of—the investment. No investment, whether performing or not, should be purchased or acquired without a clear understanding of the exit strategy.

There are some assets—notes and deeds—that have immediate value, some with cash flow and many without, and therefore have a different exit strategy than those that require additional capital to reposition, complete construction or entitlement, or are dormant and have a calculated hold period and cost.

As discussed earlier, the hold period is a critical element in analyzing the acquisition and disposition of the asset and is usually hand-in-glove with the exit strategy.

Value in Leases

For the purpose of discussion and within the realm of distressed assets, the value of the lease is a measure of safety and yield. The stronger the tenant the more likely the terms of the lease will be kept and thus purchasing an asset at discount will increase the value of the asset to the buyer. A credit tenant such as Kohl's, Wal-Mart, McDonalds, etc. are known to be credit tenants often with corporate guarantees even if the property is vacated. Local tenants such as Billy's Dry Cleaners are at best only as good as the last payment received and therefore the stronger the tenant the less the risk. Distressed assets that have leases would be valued based on the income, terms, and pass through (property tax, insurance, maintenance, common area maintenance (CAM)). Lease values are used to calculate the return or yield. Depending on the value of the lease and the discount on the asset value (note or deed) will determine the net benefit of holding the asset. Additionally, determining the lease up value on vacant or value added real estate will determine the future value or current discount of the asset.

Guarantee

As I've mentioned throughout this book, there is a difference between residential (including two to four units) and commercial. For the sake of discussion, we will focus on the commercial aspects for this section and for most of this chapter. Often, the note purchase will include the entire file, including corporate or personal guarantees. This could be a valuable cushion, added yield, or leverage to the acquisition of the note. Even sophisticated brokers and investors forget to add value to the note for guarantees. Some discount the value of the guarantee even before analyzing if there is any value when the difference of the guarantee for margin or yield would make the note that much more valuable. Some lenders may keep the guarantee and carve out the asset secured by the note, and thus provide an added discount, keeping the guarantee. The guarantee may also include cross-collateral, in which the borrower would find a way to re-write the note with additional conditions or modifications so that the cross-collateral is not in jeopardy. All of these options are important to identify up front so that the true value of the note, asset value, and conditions can be analyzed for optimum reward and minimal risk.

Surprises

Surprises are unknowns not assessed during due diligence. Know ahead of time that there will be surprises. No matter how well you may plan for the inevitable, also plan for surprises. The list may be divided into known and unknown variables, which often will be uncovered during the time of due diligence.

One of the most effective ways to plan for surprises is to do a FAQ. Be a "devil's advocate," and assume everything will go wrong at some time in the plan. Check off the known or secured elements of the plan; what is left over should limit the surprises. Plan anyway, including such precautions as a cushion reserve, longer hold period, added cost for sales and marketing, lower resale prices, and lower cap return.

I often run into the same people over and over again who have expectations based on luck, only to hear a year later it didn't pan out. Having realistic expectations is a foundation for successful investment of any kind. "Under-promise, over-deliver" is a recipe for success.

Now, that's not to say a deal won't drop into your lap at some point in time, but again, this is part of the risk/reward timeline.

Learn some of the basics to assess risk/reward choices. By that, I mean learn the terms and calculations, and understand the impact on your investment. Here are my Baker's Dozen of Basics:

What	Why	Reason
1. Income	Potential of income	Income to meet obligations and insure for the return of and return on capital
2. Expenses	Assess the exposure for operating expense	Be sure to include all expenses, management, reserves, repairs, travel
3. Net Income	Profit	Must be real and not estimated or reduced for seller perks. Match to tax returns.
4. Cap Rate	Capitalization Rate, Return on capital	Initial rate of return based on purchase price, value add, or forecast
5. DSCR	Debt Service Cover Ratio	Cushion to meet the obligations of the debt service based on interest and/or P&I
6. IRR	Internal Rate of Return	Actual measurement of financial benefit
7. Cash on Cash	Return on capital net of leverage	Ultimate return net of debt service and leverage
8. Depreciation	Tax benefits	Benefit of real estate ownership to reduce taxes
9. Leverage	Loan, debt, or use of other funds for acquisition	Using financing to increase net return with a risk of debt service
10. Management	Oversight or service to maintain and operate investment	Most important other than cash and reserves
11. LTV	Loan to value used to determine margin of equity	Measurement of value net of equity
12. Lease Type	Level of responsibility	The more obligations to the tenant lessee, the less the risk of debt service
13. Resources	Capital, third-party services, legal, tax, safety net	Collection of capital services, and necessary services to maintain & preserve value

Table 4: Baker's Dozen of Basics

I have a saying: "There's always a reason not to do the deal." When the risk outweighs the reward, the deal will not close. Every buyer has his or her risk/reward assessment criteria. Weigh your risk/reward using some of the following strategies:

1. Cash flow

2. Safety factors

3. Liquidity

4. Return of capital

5. Return on capital

6. Time frame on holding

7. Acquisition strategy

8. Exit strategy

9. What if

10. Level of understanding

11. Level of knowledge

12. Capital limits

13. Leverage

Summary of Chapter:

Like any decision in life, there are choices to be made based on our knowledge, experience, risk tolerance, motivation, fallback plan, and a myriad of other variables. In distressed real estate, there are additional expectations and risks. The expectations are higher due to the quest for a bargain, above-average discount, and greed to make a profit far beyond that of a retail, cash flow, or other safe investment. Other than liquidity, there is really no difference between those who buy T-Bills or government-insured bonds and those who want an annualized return of 12 percent, 18 percent, 24 percent, or higher returns, except that the latter have a higher risk tolerance and therefore may cash in on their plan.

> **"I don't think much of a man who is not wiser today than he was yesterday."** —*Abraham Lincoln*

CHAPTER ELEVEN

Truth or Consequences

So, I'm going to ask for a little indulgence as I set the stage. Although the concept of truth is as old and tested as mankind, at no other time in modern business history has the truth become more adverse than it is now, and in the end, the consequences of ignoring it are more costly than ever.

In the early days of television, there was a famous quiz show called "Truth or Consequences."[1] Originally hosted on NBC radio by Ralph Edwards (1940-'57) and later on television by Bob Barker (1956-'75), the concept was the same: Answer the truth or ... take the consequences. The television show ran on CBS, NBC, and also in syndication. The premise of the show was to mix the original quiz element of game shows with wacky stunts.

On the show, people had to answer a trivia question correctly (usually an off-the-wall question that no one would be able to answer correctly, or a bad joke) and had about two seconds to do so before "Beulah the Buzzer" was sounded. (On the rare occasion that the contestant answered the question correctly before Beulah was heard, another question was asked.)

If the contestant could not complete the "truth" portion, there would be "consequences"—usually a zany and embarrassing stunt. From the start, most contestants preferred to answer the question wrong in order to perform the stunt. Said Edwards, "Most of the American people are darned good sports." During Barker's run as host, the game "Barker's Box" was played. Barker's Box was a box with four drawers in it. A contestant who was able to pick the drawer with money in it won a bonus prize.

The show has a lot in common with cashing in on distressed assets in a down market. If you do not sift through superficial presentations, and instead assume you are getting the truth (or "take their word for it"), you may experience the negative consequences.

Ask for Proof of Funds (POF)

Sounds pretty basic, but think of the consequences if you don't have the truth during a transaction. As a broker, buy/sell representative, referral, title representative, or even the direct seller, what would happen if you were to put in all the time to vet (covered in Chapter Nine) only to find out there is no source of funds to close?

Now, some purchases require all cash up front; others will be subject to financing or other arrangement outlined in the LOI or purchase agreement that the parties have agreed to up front. However, those sources also need to be verified (i.e., POF) within the expectations of the parties.

POF can be in the form of a bank letter with invitation to contact, so all the personal contact information needs to be available. Be careful of those letters because sometimes in a letter of credit (LOC) the contact information is blocked out and cannot be verified. This is sometimes called a soft proof of funds (soft POF), but the message here is that if the buyer is saying he has the funds, then the LOC—or commitment of funding—should be verifiable. There is value in a soft POF in that if certain information is visible (date, dollar amount, "good through" date, and a signature and title), the soft POF could be used as an indicative bid or an "I'll take the first step" to set up the intent.

Be cautious of anyone asking for a hard POF without some indication of product, price, or control. It is a common mistake to ask for a hard POF and blind LOI (letter of intent with open and undefined terms) as a ticket to shop a deal. Although there are some who say it can be done, I would err on the side of caution in that we have never heard of a deal closing with such a protocol. Use common sense with this claim, and save yourself the time, cost, credibility, and aggravation by not buying into that scheme. If you do buy in and take the plunge, expect to see your POF used by others to shop your deal, or even worse, to lock down an asset, pool, or tape.

POF should only be verified bank-to-bank or seller-to-bank. Anyone acting as an "agent" to verify funds should be able to back it up in writing from an authorized source—either the same or a third-party source.

Vet the Asset, Seller, and Buyer

As discussed in the previous chapters, vetting is a process to verify the facts. This is probably the most important action item and needs to be done before any additional effort is invested into the offering.

Vetting the product is in some way the same process as vetting the seller. If the product is vetted by making sure the seller is the named entity on the title or the mortgagor on a title profile or other form of seller control, then most likely the seller is vetted as a byproduct of vetting the asset. If the names are different on the title profile or other document of title, ownership, or obligation, then the second step of vetting the seller is that much more important.

We have seen situations where the asset is being promoted as "seller direct," only to find out that the seller was not the deeded owner, borrower, or direct lender. As it turned out, he was a passive investor in the asset who was planning to get a buyer under contract with no authority to convey. Fortunately for us, we discovered the level of ownership early on through the simple use of a title search. Had the discussion on form of ownership and intent been up front, we could have worked out a strategy with full disclosure (truth), as opposed to dismissing the opportunity and no longer being interested since we didn't know what other skeletons were in the closet (consequence).

On another occasion, we had a client in New York with $100 million in proofed-up funds, who was not scared of multiple closings (flips, concurrent escrow, or assignment) if disclosed up front, and the spreads were not too greedy. The problem continued to be sellers or representatives who continually swore they were the seller when they could not prove deeded ownership. Of course, often the current seller is someone who has the asset under contract as the buyer, with the intent to double-escrow or gross-up the asset. Again, in most cases a sophisticated buyer may not be turned off except for the fact that the truth was hidden, and this raises issues of credibility.

Who Are the Parties (Really)?

I touched on the parties in the previous section; however, there may be other parties in the chain of communication, and at each juncture is a weaker link, indicating that the deal will never happen. Certainly, the most likely deal scenario is a direct buyer and direct seller. The chances of each of them finding each other is rare, and therefore the industry does rely on third parties to put the deal together or at least make one party aware of the other. The problem again is a lack of truthfulness. Most of the time, other than the real buyer and the real seller, people are not who they say they are. Everyone seems to be direct—but direct to whom? Don't be surprised if you ask the person if they are the direct buyer only to find out that they are direct TO the buyer. The same may hold true for the sell side. I can't tell you why there is this infidelity in the distressed asset segment as a general observation, but I assume it has something to do with validating the fees or protecting their source.

Another strange phenomenon is a situation in which the buyer may also be a broker, and therefore desires to position himself as the buyer sometimes and the broker for the same deal at other times. Again, if he is truly in that position, then I would press to have him be up front so that I don't do the work for the broker when he said he was the buyer. It's almost the same as when a couple comes into an open house being shown by a residential listing agent, and that agent asks the couple if they're working with someone or represented by another agent, only to find out when the offer is made that one of them is a licensed agent who is demanding a co-op. You may have been able to work the deal in a different way had you known.

We work mainly with off-market, unlisted offerings so there is no exclusive listing broker, especially on the notes; therefore, the sell side is more direct. Having said that, I caution you to be careful of independents, brokers, representatives, or unlicensed persons who claim that they control the product or seller. If that is the case, then demand a letter of authority (LOA) signed by the seller to verify such representation or right to present. In most cases, this is nothing more than a single-party listing or acknowledgement by registration of the buyer to the seller. If that cannot be obtained or is refused, then you know whom you're dealing with, and thus moving ahead has the consequence that there is either no seller or the parties are not who they present themselves to be.

When there are intermediaries, be sure they have the same authorization to represent either the buyer or the seller under the same criteria as above. In most cases, it will be a daisy chain if you are not dealing directly with the buy or sell source. The red flag is when the points or fees are grossed-up. There are several indicators in the market that will telegraph when this is occurring. We usually see a standard 3 percent or 3 points fee on transactions up to $25 million and declining fees above that amount down to 1 percent or 1 point at $100 million or higher. When we see 4 points on a deal, we know the fees are grossed-up, and there will be too many contact points that will interfere with the deal to close. Also, when the fees are 3 points on a $100 million offering, we know that this is a sham, and we will walk away.

Attorney Authorization

On some occasions, you will hear that the seller has requested the POF to be verified by the seller's attorney. As discussed previously, if this comes to your attention, be sure to get the letter of authorization. In most cases, it is an attorney participating in the daisy chain to add the façade of credibility and cut themselves in for a piece of the deal. We have found the fees to be inflated and the process delayed when this request has come into the conversation. We have also seen them use the POF for their own personal benefit by "representing" the buyer in shopping for tapes and pools, having full knowledge that the POF is good, and claiming that the original deal was no longer available, but they found another. To verify funds, we recommend only bank-to-bank POF verification OR a fully executed letter of authorization naming the attorney as the representative of the seller. Bottom line: be careful when giving your POF to anyone other than the designated authority or direct seller.

Everyone Else is a Referral

We've covered who the buyer is and who the seller is. There may be also authorized parties on both the buy and sell side by LOA. Everyone else is a referral. My point here is that a name and a number or email address is nothing more than a referral. We mentioned how fees can get grossed-up by a middleman (referral), and thus add a level of complexity and cost to the transaction. In many cases, a 1 point gross-up will jeopardize the deal altogether. Additionally, at the end of the day, one person does all the work, so other than the introduction, what is the value? This may sound like basic stuff, but it happens every day and interferes with the progress and objective in closing the deal.

Be careful of "pool and share." In the same context, there will be daisy-chain parties who suggest the fee get equally divided among all the parties. The best way to handle this scenario is to divide the direct buy and sell sides of the deal and let them determine what the introductory parties or referrals should get. This will prevent anyone from getting in the middle and will be the best strategy to get the buyer and seller as direct as possible to consummate the deal.

Brokers

There are times when brokers—both buy- and sell-side representatives—have value. Certainly, when there is an exclusive listing agreement signed by the seller designating that broker as the only authorized person to contract, there is no question. The benefit to this structure is that the sell side and representation is in writing and under contract. Even more so is the likelihood that the asset or pool is real as well, although you may still have to vet the asset as being owned or under the control of the seller.

An exclusive listing protects only the sell side relationship and requires an agreement between the listing broker and the selling broker. Do not skip this step. It can be as simple as a cooperative agreement prior to submitting the buyer's LOI or purchase agreement. Be careful not to assume that by including the agreement as part of the purchase contract, the selling broker (representing the buyer) is protected. There is no shortage of stories about cooperative brokers assuming allegiance by buyers, or handshakes with listing brokers to protect fees. In fact, it is a requirement in real estate law or by the Statute of Frauds that contracts have to be in writing to be enforceable. I'm not familiar with a single state that does not require the arrangement to be in writing.

Likewise, the buyer may have a contract, MNDA, or fee agreement with a designated representative from the buy side of the transaction. It may not be uncommon for the buyer to forget, renegotiate, or circumvent the parties. We require an MNDA and fee agreement up front so everything is disclosed, transparent, and in agreement; then we can exert every effort to close. Of course, some deals are yield- or spread-sensitive, and therefore the fees may be some type of schedule based on the actual purchase price. We just want to be sure there are no surprises or eleventh-hour fee discounts after all the work has been completed.

Intermediaries

There are instances where intermediaries are involved and facilitate putting a buyer and seller together. The difference between an intermediary and a broker is that the relationship is not one of representation. The services are generally by introduction or by consulting agreement. This may also include putting brokers together and obtaining a fee for that. Unlike the traditional agency relationship for a broker or agent to specifically represent either a buyer or a seller, there is no fiduciary for the intermediary. The intermediary represents neither the seller nor the buyer other than to be transparent and to disclose the truthful relationship. Even that, in most cases, is not disclosed. In some cases, the intermediary will provide packaging of the asset with the requirement of obtaining the necessary confidentiality agreement (CA) before releasing any pertinent information.

In most cases where there is no listing in place, and the bank, borrower, or seller want to keep a lower profile, the use of an intermediary is the middle ground to obtain interested parties. In those cases, the intermediary can serve as either the buy- or sell-side knowledge base for single or multiple opportunities.

The intermediary must not violate state law for practicing real estate without a license; he must act only as a marketing source. No contracts on behalf of others are to be prepared or executed. Consult an attorney before taking on the responsibility or preparation of any contracts that may violate applicable state law.

Performance

Has the buyer closed (i.e., performed) and has the seller delivered? I feel foolish sometimes in raising the subject, but here's one that might hit you right between the eyes. How often do we just assume that since a buyer says, "I'm an investor" or "I'm a buyer and have cash to close quickly" do we jump through hoops only to find out that their last deal was 10 years ago under completely different circumstances (market, economy, lending practices, political climate, world circumstances, and a myriad of other factors)? What I want to know is what they have closed on lately to determine expectations, tolerance, patience, requirements for cash flow or value add, reserves or asset sector; whether they closed on a note or deed; and maybe another 20 questions just to get started. My point is that it's easy to get caught up in the sale without qualifying.

A similar concept can happen with the seller, whether it is a bank, borrower, or direct seller. We track closed transactions to verify transaction activity, pricing, and timing. The reason for this is to determine whether the seller is actually transacting business. The banks in particular have not been under this kind of distress since the RTC of the late '80s and early '90s—some 20 years ago, and that was a different climate.

Summary of Chapter:

It's fitting that we wrap up with this topic since most of the book has been leading up to this subject. The whole purpose of this book is to share my experiences and to help save you time and money—lots of time and lots of money. Putting in the time to vet the asset, buyer, and seller will pay off big dividends in analyzing the opportunity and assessing the risk/reward. The best way to get off to the right start is to uncover the truth. Seems pretty basic, and in most cases I'm sure the information is accurate; however, this is no time to be trusting. The increase in opportunity for brokers, representatives, attorney, intermediaries, buyers, and sellers has muddied the real deal; therefore, I suggest being less trusting and more factual with vetting the asset, process, protocol, and buyers and sellers to get to the truth—or pay the consequences.

References:

1. Wikipedia: en.Wikipedia.org/wiki/Truth_or_Consequences.

CHAPTER TWELVE

Frequently Asked Questions

"Doesn't buying discounted debt entail a high level of risk, especially on non-performing debt?"

Buying debt at a discount is much like any other investment or commodity. Buying at a discount provides an immediate hedge against risk. Buying at a discount (20 to 80 percent, depending on the asset) provides a margin for profit. Each note has a unique strategy to acquire or exit.

"What is the risk, and how is my money protected?"

Funds are either for direct purchase or as a member of a LLC. The LLC owns the note or converted asset, and investors own a proportional share of the LLC, much like stockholders. The LLC has rules and controls to ensure the investor understands the risk, benefits, and payouts. Usually in an LLC or private placement, there are operating fees, and the next dollar out to the investors is either as return of principal, preferred return on investment, or profit share. No true investment can guarantee that nothing will happen to an investor's funds, but if the controls and expectations are managed from the beginning, then the risk can be mitigated and reduced.

"Sounds too good to be true. How can I be sure the asset can be sold and I will get legal title?"

Too good to be true is a matter of expectation. In the debt recovery market, 20 to 60 percent or more is not uncommon, but rarely presented to the private investor. Some use in-house and third-party asset managers who have expertise in asset management, loss recovery, forbearance, modification, property management, investor relations, and operations. Some investors will choose to acquire the note or deed and will require due diligence (covered in Chapter Six). If you are not versed in due diligence, be sure to hire the proper experts to minimize and eliminate unknown risk.

"Am I personally responsible to pay off any debt when I purchase the Note?"

No. The asset is the debt if you were to purchase the note intact with all the terms originally agreed to in advance by the borrower. In some cases, there may be enough cash flow or margin on the note that financing would increase the yield, and therefore only the note is the collateral. This makes the investment an ideal purchase for an IRA/401(k) in that the gains are deferred in the retirement account and the debt is paid by the LLC.

"I want income to make sure the investment is making the kind of return I expect. Is this income?"

In most cases, the answer is yes. Depending on the strategy of the purchase and exit, the note will produce an income based on the face value of the note or its modified terms. Performing notes, of course, will provide a cash flow distributed based on proportional ownership. Non-performing notes may require some modification or hold for an exit disposition, which may include selling to a secondary market, foreclosure, or resale to the original borrower.

"What form of ownership should I use?"

Always seek professional tax and legal advice before making any investment with which you are not familiar. This includes notes and deeds, especially distressed assets, as they usually have some risk—both present and future. Ownership can take many forms ranging from personal, corporation, LLC, partnerships, and various combinations. Although it mainly depends on where the funds are coming from, debt and responsibility obligations, and tax considerations, most single asset ownership is in the form of a single asset LLC since this will shield the asset and liability. Gains and losses are passed on to the individual owners (members). Seek appropriate tax and legal advice to discuss your options.

"How do the cycles of real estate affect the market?"

Like other markets (e.g., stock market, precious metals) real estate is cyclical. Buy low and sell high or sell high and buy low. Either strategy provides a margin of profit or spread. Timing the market is not a good strategy and requires more luck than skill. Understanding the peaks and valleys can mitigate the risk. No doubt, the current economic crisis that began in mid- to late-2007 provides an excellent example of the cyclical market in that there has been a bottom, middle, and top of the market. It is easier to track a market that is rising than one that is going down. Compare the spread (risk) of buying while it's going down to that of when it is going up to determine the cost of waiting or acting.

"What are distressed assets?"

At the highest level, "distressed" refers to condition, just as "perfect" denotes a condition. In the past, "distressed" referred to physically or economically depressed assets. But since the recent financial downturn, the word "distressed" refers primarily to the financial condition, not necessarily the physical condition level of obsolescence.

"Is it a note or a deed?"

Understanding what is being bought or offered is the first step. Sophisticated investors want the notes because they have multiple exit strategies. Deeds, including short pay, REO, and pre-foreclosures, are for investors who require the deed for ownership. This could be due to the need to refinance, leverage the purchase, or hold as equity; the terms of a syndication; covenants; exit strategies; and other reasons to have ownership recorded as a deed (1031 is an example of a "like kind" deed).

"Why are distressed assets seldom listed?"

There are a number of reasons why a distressed asset is not listed. The bank may not own it yet, as in the case of a note. In circumstances where there is more than one lender—also referred to as participation—getting all the participating banks to agree may not be easy. Also, the bank does not want to pay the fee. On a traditional commercial listing, in an exclusive listing agreement the owner is responsible for paying a fee that may reduce the net transaction to the bank. The bank does not want others to know of its misjudgment and embarrassment. Listing brokers are required to disclose everything known, which may include information the lender is not aware of or even liable for. Lastly, listed properties seldom have the sense of urgency that non-listed or off-market assets possess.

"What is an NDA and why is it used?"

The non-disclosure agreement (NDA), often called a non-circumvent or (NCA), mutual NDA (MNDA) or confidentiality agreement (CA), is used to prevent the dissemination and transfer of non-public information. It is also used to make sure the parties do not circumvent, meaning they do not "go around" rules and laws to avoid paying a fee or getting a client that is not agreed to in advance. Since distressed assets are usually not listed under an exclusive listing agreement where the seller pays the fee, the fee is paid by the buyer/investor. This requires what is often referred to as a buyer-broker agreement or similar agreement whereby the buyer agrees to pay the fee. Disclosing the location, address, APN, or other identity before an agreement is reached would allow the buyer rep or buyer to circumvent the procuring source and not be obligated to pay a fee.

Often, the asset is not disclosed until the NDA is signed, due in part to the likelihood that there may be third parties (agents, other brokers, or other buyers) who would share the information without consideration for the damage that may be caused to owners, borrowers, brokers, lenders, and the like. In order for business to operate based on the intent of all the parties, an NDA is usually the first step in the process of building a relationship.

"Why is there not a complete package like those on the MLS?"

The lender and borrower are usually at odds, if not by evidence, then simply by the fact that there is a lender and a borrower in trouble. The borrower is not meeting the borrowing obligations, and the lender has a fiduciary responsibility to its stockholders and the state and federal examiners for transparency. Unlike a retail-listed commercial transaction, the lender does not have updated financials within the past year, and the asset is not being offered by the borrower. Even if the bank has a receiver, asset manager, or property manager under contract, that does not mean the financial documents will be volunteered before contract. Appraisals are often done by the banks when an asset is in trouble; however, such appraisals are paid for by the bank and are the property of the bank. If a note is being purchased, that would be in the file to be reviewed upon an accepted purchase contract.

"Is it true that the buyer pays the fee? Who determines the rate?"

Since the lender, bank, or seller is taking the beating on the discount, writing down the asset, and taking the markdown, they will pass any fees to the buyer. Additionally, in most cases, the bank or seller will not give a listing agreement, which does not mean that the buyer cannot request that the fee be paid by the seller. Since the assets are discounted to the market, so are the fees. The baseline for buyer-paid fees begins at 3 percent. On transactions of larger amounts—$25 million or higher—the fee could go down to 1 percent to be shared by all parties.

"What is a 'daisy chain,' and how does it affect the transaction?"

A daisy chain refers to multiple parties (e.g., brokers, intermediaries, referrals) in the deal. In a retail transaction, only the listing broker is entitled to a fee based on a listing agreement (e.g., exclusive, open, single-party, net). It is based on the listing broker's advance agreement with others as to whether the fee will be shared or "co-op." In distressed assets, when there is no exclusive listing agreement, the parties need to have the arrangement, often termed "paper up," before the parties reveal their buyer and seller. Rarely, if ever, is there only one broker direct from the seller to the buyer. And rarely is there only one seller rep direct to a buyer rep. If that were the case, the fee may be shared 50/50. In most cases, there are at least three touch points: a seller rep, an intermediary (middle broker), and a buyer rep.

To compound the problem, there is usually little, if anything, known about the direct seller or buyer, and seldom are these transactions completed. The market often relies on referrals to bring a property or buyer to the market. Where the scheme goes awry is the expectation that a pool-and-share distribution is best for all parties. There are numerous strategies and fee structures that can address the fees, but seldom will a daisy chain result in closing a transaction unless there is complete transparency from the beginning.

"What is the best way to get my offer accepted and at my price?"

In the traditional retail or commercial deal, the buyer makes an offer as low as possible with the sole objective to see how low the seller would go by virtue of a counteroffer. Unfortunately, in today's distressed and discounted marketplace, many lenders will not respond with counteroffers to test the "how low will they go" strategy. On the contrary, it is more advisable to get their attention with an offer that is closer to the strike price and make quantifiable adjustments during the due diligence period. An insulting offer may even disqualify the buyer in that they may not be taken seriously by the lender. Finally, to get the offer accepted, it is helpful to know what makes lenders separate the amateurs from the serious buyers. Having a company profile, a short plan of acquisition and exit, proof of funds, and professional LOI is critical in getting noticed from the start and being taken seriously.

GLOSSARY

absorption: The amount of inventory or units of a specific commercial property type that become occupied during a specified time period (usually a year) in a given market, typically reported as the absorption rate.

acceleration clause: A clause in your mortgage that allows the lender to demand payment of the outstanding loan balance for various reasons. The most common reasons for accelerating a loan are if the borrower defaults on the loan or transfers title to another individual without informing the lender.

adjustable-rate mortgage (ARM): A mortgage in which the interest changes periodically, according to corresponding fluctuations in an index. All ARMs are tied to indexes.

adjustment date: The date the interest rate changes on an adjustable-rate mortgage.

amortization: The loan payment consists of a portion that will be applied to pay the accruing interest on a loan, with the remainder being applied to the principal. Over time, the interest portion decreases as the loan balance decreases, and the amount applied to the principal increases so that the loan is paid off (amortized) in the specified time.

amortization schedule: A table that shows how much of each payment will be applied toward principal and how much toward interest over the life of the loan. It also shows the gradual decrease of the loan balance until it reaches zero.

annual percentage rate (APR): A value created according to a government formula intended to reflect the true annual cost of borrowing, expressed as a percentage. This is not the note rate on your loan. To roughly calculate APR, use this formula as a guideline: deduct the closing costs from your loan amount, then, using your actual loan payment, calculate what the interest rate would be on this amount instead of your actual loan amount. You will come up with a number close to the APR. Because you are using the same payment on a smaller amount, the APR is always higher than the actual note rate on your loan.

application: The form used to apply for a mortgage loan, containing information about a borrower's income, savings, assets, and debts.

appraisal: Written justification of the price paid for a property, primarily based on an analysis of comparable sales of similar homes nearby.

appraised value: An opinion of a property's fair market value, based on an appraiser's knowledge, experience, and analysis of the property. Since an appraisal is primarily based on comparable sales, and the most recent sale is the one on the property in question, the appraisal usually comes out at the purchase price.

appraiser: An individual qualified by education, training, and experience to estimate the value of real property and personal property. Although some appraisers work directly for mortgage lenders, most are independent.

appreciation: The increase in the value of a property due to changes in market conditions, inflation, or other causes.

assessed value: The valuation placed on property by a public tax assessor for purposes of taxation.

assessor: A public official who establishes the value of a property for taxation purposes.

asset: An item of value owned by an individual. Assets that can be quickly converted into cash are considered "liquid assets." These include bank accounts, stocks, bonds, and mutual funds. Other assets include real estate, personal property, and debts owed to an individual by others.

asset manager: Broadly defined, refers to any system whereby things that are of value to an entity or group are monitored and maintained—for the purpose of distressed assets, usually a bank official, receiver, or trustee. Specific asset managers may take responsibility for physical property management and financial management, as well as construction and loss mitigation. The asset manager does not necessarily have final disposition authority, but may influence the decision.

assignment: The process by which ownership of your mortgage is transferred from one company or individual to another. The result of that process is also called an assignment.

assumable mortgage: A mortgage that can be assumed by the buyer when a home is sold. Usually, the borrower must "qualify" in order to assume the loan.

balloon mortgage: A mortgage loan that requires the remaining principal balance be paid at a specific point in time. For example, a loan may be amortized as if it would be paid over a 30-year period, but requires that at the end of the 10th year the entire remaining balance must be paid.

balloon payment: The final lump sum payment that is due at the termination of a balloon mortgage.

bankruptcy: The result of an individual or individuals restructuring or relieving themselves of debts and liabilities by filing in federal bankruptcy court. Bankruptcies are of various types, but the most common for an individual seem to be a "Chapter 7 No Asset" bankruptcy which relieves the borrower of most types of unsecured debts. A borrower cannot usually qualify for an "A" paper loan for a period of two years after the bankruptcy has been discharged and requires the reestablishment of an ability to repay debt.

bridge loan: A short-term loan, used to bridge the gap. For example, a loan used to buy a property until a permanent loan can be secured is a bridge loan.

broker opinion of value (BOV): Used in the commercial market for general value from a commercial broker; usually includes an estimate of income and capitalization value.

broker price opinion (BPO): Used primarily in the residential market to determine an opinion, not an appraised value, of the comparative value; also referred to as a "drive-by" value.

cap: Adjustable-rate mortgages have fluctuating interest rates, but those fluctuations are usually limited to a certain amount. Those limitations may apply to how much the loan may adjust over a six-month period, an annual period, and over the life of the loan, and are referred to as "caps." Some ARMs, although they may have a life cap, allow the interest rate to fluctuate freely, but require a certain minimum payment that can change once a year. There is a limit on how much that payment can change each year, and that limit is also referred to as a cap.

capital expenditures: Property improvements that cannot be expensed as a current operating expense for tax purposes.

capitalization rate (cap rate): The ratio between the net operating income produced by an *asset* and its *capital cost* (the original *price* paid to buy the asset) or, alternatively, its current *market value*. This is usually the number-one factor to determining value and its relationship to income and return potential. Cap rate is calculated by net income (NOI)/price. Cap rate is also used to determine a price point base on a return rate by the formula: net income (NOI/cap rate) = price.

cash flow: The net cash received in any period, taking into account net operating income, debt service, capital expenses, loan proceeds, sale revenues, and any other sources and uses of cash.

cash-on-cash rate: A return measure that is calculated as cash flow before taxes divided by the initial equity investment.

cash-out refinance: The result of a borrower refinancing his mortgage at a higher amount than the current loan balance with the intention of pulling out money for personal use.

chain of title: An analysis of the transfers of title to a piece of property over time.

clear title: A title that is free of liens or legal questions as to ownership of the property.

closing: This has different meanings in different states. In some states, a real estate transaction is not consider "closed" until the documents record at the local recorder's office. In others, the "closing" is a meeting where all of the documents are signed and money changes hands.

cloud on title: Any conditions revealed by a title search that adversely affect the title to real estate. Usually clouds on title cannot be removed except by deed, release, or court action.

co-borrower: An additional individual who is both obligated on the loan and is on the title to the property.

collateral: An asset that a borrower risks losing if a loan is not repaid according to the terms of the mortgage or deed of trust. In a home loan, the property is the collateral.

community property: Property that is considered to be owned jointly by a married couple, except under special circumstances. Community property only applies in some states, (e.g., Southwestern states) and is an outgrowth of the Spanish and Mexican heritage of the area.

comparable sales: Recent sales of similar properties in nearby areas. Used to help determine the market value of a property; also referred to as "comps."

condominium: A type of ownership in real property whereby all of the owners own the property, common areas, and buildings together, with the exception of the interior of the unit to which they have title. Often mistakenly referred to as a type of construction or development, a condominium actually refers to the type of ownership.

construction loan: A short-term, interim loan for financing the cost of construction. The lender makes payments to the builder at periodic intervals as the work progresses.

contingency: A condition that must be met before a contract is legally binding. For example, home purchasers often include a contingency specifying that the contract is not binding until the purchaser obtains a satisfactory home inspection report from a qualified home inspector.

conventional mortgage: Refers to home loans other than government loans (VA and FHA).

convertible ARM: An adjustable-rate mortgage that allows the borrower to change the ARM to a fixed-rate mortgage within a specific time.

cooperative (co-op): A type of multiple ownership in which the residents of a multiunit housing complex own shares in the cooperative corporation that owns the property, giving each resident the right to occupy a specific apartment or unit.

credit history: A record of an individual's repayment of debt. Credit histories are reviewed by mortgage lenders as one of the underwriting criteria in determining credit risk.

creditor: A person to whom money is owed.

credit report: A report of an individual's credit history prepared by a credit bureau and used by a lender in determining a loan applicant's creditworthiness.

debt: An amount owed to another.

debt-coverage ratio (DCR): Sometimes referred to as debt service coverage ratio (DSCR), this is the ratio or net operating income to annual debt service; it is expressed as net operating income divided by annual debt service.

deed: The legal document conveying title to a property (e.g., grant deed, warranty deed, quitclaim deed).

deed-in-lieu: Short for "deed in lieu of foreclosure," this conveys title to the lender when the borrower is in default and wants to avoid foreclosure. The lender may or may not cease foreclosure activities if a borrower asks to provide a deed-in-lieu. Regardless of whether the lender accepts the deed-in-lieu, the avoidance and non-repayment of debt will most likely show on a credit history. What a deed-in-lieu may prevent is having the documents preparatory to a foreclosure recorded and becoming a matter of public record.

deed of trust: Essentially the same as a mortgage. Used in some states, such as California, that do not record mortgages.

default: Failure to make the mortgage payment within a specified period of time. For first mortgages or first trust deeds, if a payment has still not been made within 30 days of the due date, the loan is considered to be in default.

depreciation: Decline in the value of property; the opposite of appreciation. Depreciation is also an accounting term that shows the declining monetary value of an asset and is used as an expense to reduce taxable income. Since this is not a true expense where money is actually paid, lenders will add back depreciation expense for self-employed borrowers and count it as income.

distressed asset: Formerly associated with only physical or economic obsolescence, the term is now more closely associated with negative financial condition, incomplete construction, or over-encumbrance.

down payment: The part of the purchase price of a property that the buyer pays in cash and does not finance with a mortgage.

due diligence: The process of examining a property, related documents, and procedures conducted by or for the potential lender or purchaser to reduce risk. Applying a consistent standard of inspection and investigation can determine whether actual conditions reflect the information represented.

due-on-sale provision: A provision in a mortgage that allows the lender to demand repayment in full if the borrower sells the property that serves as security for the mortgage.

easement: A right-of-way giving persons other than the owner access to or over a property.

eminent domain: The right of a government to take private property for public use upon payment of its fair market value. Eminent domain is the basis for condemnation proceedings.

encroachment: An improvement that intrudes illegally on another's property.

encumbrance: Anything that affects or limits the fee simple title to a property, such as mortgages, leases, easements, or restrictions.

Equal Credit Opportunity Act (ECOA): A federal law that requires lenders and other creditors to make credit equally available without discrimination based on race, color, religion, national origin, age, sex, marital status, or receipt of income from public assistance programs.

equity: A homeowner's financial interest in a property. Equity is the difference between the fair market value of the property and the amount still owed on its mortgage and other liens.

escrow: An item of value, money, or documents deposited with a third party, to be delivered upon the fulfillment of a condition. For example, the earnest money deposit is put into escrow until delivered to the seller when the transaction is closed.

escrow account: Once you close your purchase transaction, you may have an escrow account or impound account with your lender. This means the amount you pay each month includes an amount above what would be required if you were only paying your principal and interest. The extra money is held in your impound account (escrow account) for the payment of items like property taxes and homeowner's insurance when they come due. The lender pays them with your money instead of you paying them yourself.

eviction: The lawful expulsion of an occupant from real property.

exchange: Real estate traded for other like-kind property. Under Section 1031 of the Internal Revenue Code, like-kind property used in a trade or business or held as an investment can be exchanged with all capital gains taxes deferred until the newly acquired real estate is disposed of in a taxable transaction.

exclusive listing: A written contract that gives a licensed real estate agent the exclusive right to sell a property for a specified time.

executor: A person named in a will to administer an estate. The court will appoint an administrator if no executor is named. "Executrix" is the feminine form.

expenses: Relative costs associated with ownership.

Fair Credit Reporting Act: A consumer protection law that regulates the disclosure of consumer credit reports by consumer/credit reporting agencies and establishes procedures for correcting mistakes on one's credit record.

fair market value: The highest price that a buyer, willing but not compelled to buy, would pay, and the lowest a seller, willing but not compelled to sell, would accept.

Fannie Mae (FNMA): The Federal National Mortgage Association, which is a congressionally chartered, shareholder-owned company that is the nation's largest supplier of home mortgage funds. For a discussion of the roles of Fannie Mae, Freddie Mac (FHLMC), and Ginnie Mae (GNMA), see FreddieMac.com, FannieMae.com, or GinnieMae.gov.

Federal Housing Administration (FHA): An agency of the U.S. Department of Housing and Urban Development (HUD). Its main activity is the insuring of residential mortgage loans made by private lenders. The FHA sets standards for construction and underwriting but does not lend money or plan or construct housing.

fee simple: The greatest possible interest a person can have in real estate.

fee simple estate: An unconditional, unlimited estate of inheritance that represents the greatest estate and most extensive interest in land that can be enjoyed. It is of perpetual duration. When the real estate is in a condominium project, the unit owner is the exclusive owner only of the air space within his or her portion of the building (the unit) and is an owner in common with respect to the land and other common portions of the property.

FHA mortgage: Mortgage that is insured by the Federal Housing Administration (FHA). Along with VA loans, an FHA loan will often be referred to as a government loan.

firm commitment: A lender's agreement to make a loan to a specific borrower on a specific property.

first mortgage: The mortgage that is in first place among any loans recorded against a property. Usually refers to the date in which loans are recorded, but there are exceptions.

fixed-rate mortgage: Mortgage in which the interest rate does not change during the entire term of the loan.

fixture: Personal property that becomes real property when attached in a permanent manner to real estate.

flood insurance: Insurance that compensates for physical property damage resulting from flooding. It is required for properties located in federally designated flood areas.

foreclosure: The legal process by which a borrower in default under a mortgage is deprived of his or her interest in the mortgaged property. This usually involves a forced sale of the property at public auction with the proceeds of the sale being applied to the mortgage debt.

Government National Mortgage Association (Ginnie Mae): A government-owned corporation within the U.S. Department of Housing and Urban Development (HUD). Created by Congress on September 1, 1968, GNMA performs the same role as Fannie Mae and Freddie Mac in providing funds to lenders for making home loans. The difference is that Ginnie Mae provides funds for government loans (FHA and VA).

grantee: The person to whom an interest in real property is conveyed.

grantor: The person conveying an interest in real property.

GRM (gross rent multiplier): A method investors may use to determine market value. It calculates the market value of a property by using the gross rents an investor anticipates the property will produce at end of year one, multiplied by a given factor by dividing the price by the gross income.

hazard insurance: Insurance coverage in the event of physical damage to a property from fire, wind, vandalism, or other hazards.

home equity line of credit: A mortgage loan, usually in second position, that allows the borrower to obtain cash drawn against the equity of his home, up to a predetermined amount.

home inspection: A thorough inspection by a professional that evaluates the structural and mechanical condition of a property. A satisfactory home inspection is often included as a contingency by the purchaser.

homeowners' association: A nonprofit association that manages the common areas of a planned unit development (PUD) or condominium project. In a condominium project, it has no ownership interest in the common elements. In a PUD project, it holds title to the common elements.

homeowner's insurance: An insurance policy that combines personal liability insurance and hazard insurance coverage for a dwelling and its contents.

homeowner's warranty: A type of insurance often purchased by homebuyers that will cover repairs to certain items, such as heating or air conditioning, should they break down within the coverage period. The buyer often requests the seller to pay for this coverage as a condition of the sale, but either party can pay.

HUD-1 settlement statement: A document that provides an itemized listing of the funds that were paid at closing. Items that appear on the statement include real estate commissions, loan fees, points, and initial escrow (impound) amounts. Each type of expense goes on a specific numbered line on the sheet. The totals at the bottom of the HUD-1 statement define the seller's net proceeds and the buyer's net payment at closing. It is called a HUD1 because the form is printed by the Department of Housing and Urban Development (HUD). The HUD1 statement is also known as the "closing statement" or "settlement sheet."

income: Receipts and revenue from business or rent. Gross income includes all income, effective income may include other income, and net income is less all relative expenses.

income capitalization approach: A method to estimate the value of an income-producing property by converting net operating income into a value. It is calculated by dividing net operating income by capitalization rate.

Internal Rate of Return (IRR): a *rate of return* used in *capital budgeting* to measure and compare the *profitability* of *investments*. It is also called the *discounted cash flow* rate of return.

joint tenancy: A form of ownership or taking title to property, which means that each party owns the whole property and that ownership is not separate. In the event of the death of one party, the survivor owns the property in its entirety.

judgment: A decision made by a court of law. In judgments that require the repayment of a debt, the court may place a lien against the debtor's real property as collateral for the judgment's creditor.

judicial foreclosure: A type of foreclosure proceeding used in some states that is handled as a civil lawsuit and conducted entirely under the auspices of a court. Other states use non-judicial foreclosure.

jumbo loan: A loan that exceeds Fannie Mae's and Freddie Mac's loan limits, currently at $417,000; also called a nonconforming loan. Freddie Mac and Fannie Mae loans are referred to as conforming loans.

late charge: The penalty a borrower must pay when a payment is made after a stated number of days. On a first trust deed or mortgage, this is usually 15 days.

lease: A written agreement between the property owner and a tenant that stipulates the payment and conditions under which the tenant may possess the real estate for a specified period of time.

leasehold estate: A way of holding title to a property wherein the mortgagor does not actually own the property but rather has a recorded long-term lease on it.

lease option: An alternative financing option that allows homebuyers to lease a home with an option to buy. Each month's rent payment may consist of not only the rent, but also an additional amount which can be applied toward the down payment on an already specified price.

legal description: A property description, recognized by law, that is sufficient to locate and identify the property without oral testimony.

lender: A term that can refer to the institution making the loan or to the individual representing the firm. For example, loan officers are often referred to as "lenders."

liabilities: A person's financial obligations. Liabilities include long-term and short-term debt, as well as any other amounts that are owed to others.

liability insurance: Insurance coverage that offers protection against claims alleging that a property owner's negligence or inappropriate action resulted in bodily injury or property damage to another party. It is usually part of a homeowner's insurance policy.

lien: Legal claim against a property that must be paid off when the property is sold. A mortgage or first trust deed is considered a lien.

line of credit: An agreement by a commercial bank or other financial institution to extend credit up to a certain amount for a certain time to a specified borrower.

liquid asset: Cash asset or an asset that is easily converted into cash.

loan: A sum of borrowed money (principal) that is generally repaid with interest.

loan officer: Also referred to by a variety of other terms, such as lender, loan representative, loan "rep," account executive, and others. The loan officer serves several functions and has various responsibilities including soliciting loans, representing the lending institutions, and representing the borrower to the lending institution.

loan origination: How a lender refers to the process of obtaining new loans.

loan servicing: After you obtain a loan, the company you make the payments to is "servicing" your loan. They process payments, send statements, manage the escrow/impound account, provide collection efforts on delinquent loans, ensure that insurance and property taxes are made on the property, handle payoffs and assumptions, and provide a variety of other services.

loan-to-value (LTV): The percentage relationship between the amount of the loan and the appraised value or sales price (whichever is lower).

market data approach: A method of determining a property's value by analyzing recent sales or rental prices of comparable properties.

maturity: The date on which the principal balance of a loan, bond, or other financial instrument becomes due and payable.

merged credit report: A credit report that reports the raw data pulled from two or more of the major credit repositories. Contrast with a residential mortgage credit report (RMCR) or a standard factual credit report.

modification: Occasionally, a lender will agree to modify the terms of your mortgage without requiring you to refinance. If any changes are made, it is called a modification.

mortgage: A legal document that pledges a property to the lender as security for payment of a debt. Instead of mortgages, some states use trust deeds.

mortgage broker: A mortgage company that originates loans, then places those loans with a variety of other lending institutions, usually with whom it has preestablished relationships

mortgagee: The lender in a mortgage agreement.

mortgage insurance (MI): Insurance that covers the lender against some of the losses incurred as a result of a default on a home loan; often mistakenly referred to as PMI, which is actually the name of one of the larger mortgage insurers. Mortgage insurance is usually required in one form or another on all loans that have a loan-to-value higher than 80 percent. Mortgages above 80 percent LTV that call themselves "no MI" are usually a made at a higher interest rate. Instead of the borrower paying the mortgage insurance premiums directly, they pay a higher interest rate to the lender, who then pays the mortgage insurance themselves. Also, FHA loans and certain first-time homebuyer programs require mortgage insurance regardless of the loan-to-value.

mortgage insurance premium (MIP): The amount paid by a mortgagor for mortgage insurance, either to a government agency such as the Federal Housing Administration (FHA) or to a private mortgage insurance (MI) company.

mortgagor: The borrower in a mortgage agreement.

multi-dwelling units: Properties that provide separate housing units for more than one family, although they secure only a single mortgage.

negative amortization: Some adjustable-rate mortgages allow the interest rate to fluctuate independently of a required minimum payment. If a borrower makes the minimum payment, it may not cover all of the interest that would normally be due at the current interest rate. In essence, the borrower is deferring the interest payment, which is why this is called "deferred interest." The deferred interest is added to the balance of the loan, and the loan balance grows larger instead of smaller, which is called negative amortization.

net operating income (NOI): Equal to a property's yearly gross income less operating expenses. Gross income includes both rental income and other income such as parking fees, laundry, and vending receipts.

net present value (NPV): The sum of all future cash flows discounted to present value and netted against the initial investment.

no cash-out refinance: A refinance transaction that is not intended to put cash in the hand of the borrower. Instead, the new balance is calculated to cover the balance due on the current loan and any costs associated with obtaining the new mortgage; often referred to as a "rate and term refinance."

no-cost loan: Any lenders offer loans that you can obtain at "no cost." You should inquire whether this means there are no "lender" costs associated with the loan, or if it also covers the other costs you would normally have in a purchase or refinance transactions, such as title insurance, escrow fees, settlement fees, appraisal, recording fees, notary fees, and others. These are fees and costs that may be associated with buying a home or obtaining a loan, but not charged directly by the lender. Keep in mind that, like a "no-point" loan, the interest rate will be higher than if you obtain a loan that has costs associated with it.

non-performing: An *asset* or account of a *borrower*, which has been classified by a *bank* or *financial institution* as substandard, doubtful, or loss asset, in accordance with the directions or guidelines relating to asset classification.

note: A legal document that obligates a borrower to repay a mortgage loan at a stated interest rate during a specified period of time.

note rate: The interest rate stated on a mortgage note.

notice of default: A formal written notice to a borrower that a default has occurred and that legal action may be taken.

original principal balance: The total amount of principal owed on a mortgage before any payments are made.

origination fee: On a government loan, the loan origination fee is one percent of the loan amount, but additional points may be charged that are called "discount points." One point equals 1 percent of the loan amount. On a conventional loan, the loan origination fee refers to the total number of points a borrower pays.

owner financing: Property purchase transaction in which the property seller provides all or part of the financing.

partial payment: Payment that is not sufficient to cover the scheduled monthly payment on a mortgage loan. Normally, a lender will not accept a partial payment, but in times of hardship you can make this request of the loan servicing collection department.

par value: The stated value or face value. For a note, the par value would be the face value less any principal reductions. Some may include the late fees and accruals, but most do not.

payment change date: The date when a new monthly payment amount takes effect on an adjustable-rate mortgage (ARM) or a graduated-payment mortgage (GPM). Generally, the payment change date occurs in the month immediately after the interest rate adjustment date.

performing: Fully performing all financial responsibilities and obligations of ownership.

personal property: Any property that is not real property.

planned unit development (PUD): 1. A type of ownership where individuals actually own the building or unit they live in, but common areas are owned jointly with the other members of the development or association. Contrast with condominium, where an individual actually owns the airspace of his unit, but the buildings and common areas are owned jointly with the others in the development or association. 2. A project or subdivision that includes common property that is owned and maintained by a homeowners' association for the benefit and use of the individual PUD unit owners.

point: A point is 1 percent of the amount of the mortgage.

power of attorney: A legal document that authorizes another person to act on one's behalf. A power of attorney can grant complete authority or can be limited to certain acts and/or certain periods of time.

pre-approval: A loosely used term that is generally taken to mean that a borrower has completed a loan application and provided debt, income, and savings documentation, which an underwriter has reviewed and approved. A pre-approval is usually done at a certain loan amount and makes assumptions about what the interest rate will be at the time the loan is actually made, as well as estimates for the amount that will be paid for property taxes, insurance, and others. A pre-approval applies only to the borrower. Once a property is chosen, it must also meet the underwriting guidelines of the lender. Contrast with pre-qualification.

prepayment: Any amount paid to reduce the principal balance of a loan before the due date; payment in full on a mortgage that may result from a sale of the property, the owner's decision to pay off the loan in full, or a foreclosure. In each case, prepayment means payment occurs before the loan has been fully amortized.

prepayment penalty: A fee that may be charged to a borrower who pays off a loan before it is due.

pre-qualification: This usually refers to the loan officer's written opinion of the ability of a borrower to qualify for a home loan, after the loan officer has made inquiries about debt, income, and savings. The information provided to the loan officer may have been presented verbally or in the form of documentation, and the loan officer may or may not have reviewed a credit report on the borrower.

prime rate: The interest rate that banks charge to their preferred customers. Changes in the prime rate are widely publicized in the news media and are used as the indexes in some adjustable-rate mortgages, especially home equity lines of credit. Changes in the prime rate do not directly affect other types of mortgages, but the same factors that influence the prime rate also affect the interest rates of mortgage loans.

principal: The amount borrowed or remaining unpaid. The part of the monthly payment that reduces the remaining balance of a mortgage.

principal balance: The outstanding balance of principal on a mortgage. The principal balance does not include interest or any other charges. See "remaining balance."

principal, interest, taxes, and insurance (PITI): The four components of a monthly mortgage payment on impounded loans. Principal refers to the part of the monthly payment that reduces the remaining balance of the mortgage. Interest is the fee charged for borrowing money. Taxes and insurance refer to the amounts that are paid into an escrow account each month for property taxes and mortgage and hazard insurance.

promissory note: Written promise to repay a specified amount over a specified period of time.

purchase agreement: A written contract signed by the buyer and seller stating the terms and conditions under which a property will be sold.

quitclaim deed: A deed that transfers without warranty whatever interest or title a grantor may have at the time the conveyance is made.

real estate agent: A person licensed to negotiate and transact the sale of real estate.

Real Estate Settlement Procedures Act (RESPA): A consumer protection law that requires lenders to give borrowers disclosures and notices of closing costs.

real property: Land and appurtenances, including anything of a permanent nature such as structures, trees, minerals, and the interest, benefits, and inherent rights thereof.

Realtor®: A real estate agent, broker or an associate who holds active membership in a local real estate board that is affiliated with the National Association of Realtors.

recorder: The public official who keeps records of transactions that affect real property in the area, sometimes known as a "registrar of deeds" or "county clerk."

recording: The noting in the registrar's office of the details of a properly executed legal document, such as a deed, a mortgage note, a satisfaction of mortgage, or an extension of mortgage, thereby making it a part of the public record.

refinance transaction: The process of paying off one loan with the proceeds from a new loan using the same property as security.

remaining balance: The amount of principal that has not yet been repaid. See "principal balance."

REO (real estate owned): A property that is owned by a lender as a result of the foreclosure process. The property is held in the lender's name.

right of first refusal: A provision in an agreement that requires the owner of a property to give another party the first opportunity to purchase or lease the property before he or she offers it for sale or lease to others.

right of ingress or egress: The right to enter or leave designated premises.

right of survivorship: In joint tenancy, the right of survivors to acquire the interest of a deceased joint tenant.

sale-leaseback: A technique in which a seller deeds property to a buyer for a consideration, and the buyer simultaneously leases the property back to the seller.

second mortgage: A mortgage that has a lien position subordinate to the first mortgage.

secured loan: A loan that is backed by collateral.

security: Property that will be pledged as collateral for a loan.

seller carry-back: An agreement in which the owner of a property provides financing, often in combination with an assumable mortgage.

servicer: An organization that collects principal and interest payments from borrowers and manages borrowers' escrow accounts. The servicer often services mortgages that have been purchased by an investor in the secondary mortgage market.

servicing: The collection of mortgage payments from borrowers and related responsibilities of a loan servicer.

settlement statement: See HUD-1 settlement statement.

short sale: The process by which a lender accepts less than what he is owed on a loan he holds, where the borrower is in default.

subdivision: A housing development that is created by dividing a tract of land into individual lots for sale or lease.

subordinate financing: Any mortgage or other lien that has a priority that is lower than that of the first mortgage.

survey: A drawing or map showing the precise legal boundaries of a property, the location of improvements, easements, rights of way, encroachments, and other physical features.

sweat equity: Contribution to the construction or rehabilitation of a property in the form of labor or services rather than cash.

tenancy in common: As opposed to joint tenancy, when there are two or more individuals on title to a piece of property, this type of ownership does not pass ownership to the others in the event of death.

Texas Ratio: A measure of a bank's credit troubles. The higher the Texas Ratio, the more severe the credit troubles.

title company: A company that specializes in examining and insuring titles to real estate.

title insurance: Insurance that protects the lender (lender's policy) or the buyer (owner's policy) against loss arising from disputes over ownership of a property.

title search: A check of the title records to ensure that the seller is the legal owner of the property and that there are no liens or other claims outstanding.

transfer of ownership: Any means by which the ownership of a property changes hands. Lenders consider all of the following situations to be a transfer of ownership: the purchase of a property "subject to" the mortgage, the assumption of the mortgage debt by the property purchaser, and any exchange of possession of the property under a land sales contract or any other land trust device.

transfer tax: State or local tax payable when title passes from one owner to another.

trustee: A fiduciary who holds or controls property for the benefit of another.

Truth in Lending Act: A federal law that requires lenders to fully disclose, in writing, the terms and conditions of a mortgage, including the annual percentage rate (APR) and other charges.

unpaid balance (UPB): Outstanding loan balance or cash advance that is still due and payable. It may be the current balance on a loan, credit card account, or a past due balance, including late charges, if payments are missed. A balance unpaid more than 30 days may be reported as past due to a credit bureau.

VA mortgage: A mortgage that is guaranteed by the Department of Veterans Affairs (VA).

Veterans Administration (VA): An agency of the federal government that guarantees residential mortgages made to eligible veterans of the military services. The guarantee protects the lender against loss and thus encourages lenders to make mortgages to veterans.

yield: The percentage return on each dollar invested.

A

absorption 6, 15, 36, 84, 88, 111
acceleration 29, 111
acceleration clause 111
adjustable-rate mortgage 111, 115, 125
adjustment date 111, 125
amortization 111
amortization schedule 111
annual percentage rate 111, 129
application 49, 57, 111, 125
appraisal 11, 13-15, 26, 33, 44, 70,
    108-109, 112, 124
appraised value 112-113, 122
appraiser 5, 11, 39, 46, 112
appreciation vii, 87-88, 112, 116
APR 111, 129
ARM 111, 115, 125
ARMs 55, 111, 113
assessed value 112
assessor 112
asset iii, ix, x, 1, 3-7, 9,-11, 14-15, 17,-
    21, 23-29, 31-33, 36, 39-42, 45,
    47, 49, 53-54, 57-59, 61, 64-74,
    78, 81, 84, 87-93, 97-100, 102-
    109, 111-114, 116, 122, 124
asset manager 14, 20, 26, 32, 36, 57,
    69, 71-72, 105, 108, 112
assignment 86, 91, 99, 112
assumable mortgage 112, 128

B

balloon mortgage 112-113
balloon payment 113

bankruptcy 1, 24, 32-33, 88, 113
BOV 36, 113
BPO 14, 19, 24, 36, 55-56, 58, 70-71,
    80, 113
bridge loan 113
broker opinion of value 36, 113
broker price opinion 14, 36, 70, 113

C

cap 17, 90-91, 93, 113, 114
capital expenditures 113
capitalization rate 6, 113, 120
cap rate 17, 90, 91, 113, 114
cash flow 17, 20-21, 36, 42, 63, 74,
    87-92, 95, 103, 106, 114, 120,
    123
cash-on-cash rate 114
cash-out refinance 114, 123
chain of title 114
clear title 114
closing 5, 10, 14, 24, 28-30, 32, 36,
    40-41, 44-45, 48, 54, 57-58, 64,
    68-72, 80-81, 89, 91, 95, 98-99,
    101-103, 109, 111, 114, 117,
    120, 127
cloud on title 114
co-borrower 114
collateral 8, 9, 20, 62-63, 65, 67, 93,
    106, 114, 120, 127-128
community property 18, 114
comparable sales 112, 114
condo 12, 51
condominium 115, 118, 120, 125
construction loan 89, 63, 115
contingency 115, 119

conventional mortgage 115
convertible ARM 115
co-op 27, 51, 100, 109, 115
cooperative 102, 115
cooperative (co-op) 115
credit history 115-116
creditor 115, 117, 120
credit report 115, 118, 122, 126

D

DCR 33, 115
debt 14, 17-20, 23-24, 29, 33, 36, 42,
    44, 48, 62-63, 65, 67, 85, 87,
    89-91, 94, 105-106, 111-116,
    119-122, 125-126, 129
debt-coverage ratio (DCR) 115
deed 3, 17, 20-21, 24, 31, 36, 39, 44,
    48, 77, 88-89, 92-93, 103, 106-
    107, 114-116, 121-122, 126-127
deed-in-lieu 116
deed of trust 114, 116
default 8-9, 48, 65, 111, 116, 119,
    123-124, 128
Department of Housing and Urban
    Development 118-120
depreciation 35, 116
distressed asset iii, x, 3-5, 7, 9-11,
    24-25, 27, 29, 33, 36, 39, 59,
    66, 71, 73, 89-92, 100, 106-109,
    112, 116
down payment 36, 116, 121
due diligence iii, 8, 26, 31-32, 36,
    39-40, 42-43, 45, 49, 51, 56, 69,
    70-71, 84, 91, 93, 106, 110, 116
due-on-sale provision 116

E

easement 40-41, 43, 116-117, 128
ECOA 117
eminent domain 116-117
encroachment 39, 41, 44, 117, 128
encumbrance 24, 116-117
Equal Credit Opportunity Act
    (ECOA) 117
equity 6, 24, 27, 31, 64-66, 69, 73-74,
    79, 81, 84, 90, 94, 107, 114, 117,
    119, 126, 128
escrow 5, 20, 24, 48, 58, 71, 78, 81,
    99, 117, 120, 122, 124, 126, 128
escrow account 117, 126, 128
eviction 117
exchange ix, 12, 17-18, 65, 89, 117,
    129
exclusive listing 25, 27, 100, 102, 107-
    109, 117
executor 117
executrix 117
expenses 8, 21, 40, 42, 45, 48, 80, 87,
    94, 113-114, 116, 118, 120, 123

F

Fair Credit Reporting Act 118
fair market value 11, 55, 71, 112, 117-
    118
Fannie Mae 1, 49, 68, 73, 118-119,
    121
Federal Housing Administration
    (FHA) 118, 123
Federal National Mortgage
    Association 49, 118
fee simple 117-118
fee simple estate 118
FHA 50, 72, 83, 115, 118-119, 123
FHA mortgage 118
firm commitment 118

first mortgage 116, 118
fixed-rate mortgage 115, 119
fixture 41, 119
flood insurance 119
FNMA 49, 55, 72, 118
foreclosure 1, 5, 6, 8, 18, 20-21, 23-24, 39, 47-49, 55, 63, 65, 106-107, 116, 119, 121, 125, 127

G

Ginnie Mae 73, 118-119
Government National Mortgage Association (Ginnie Mae) 119
grantee 119
grantor 119, 126
GRM 119
gross rent multiplier 119

H

hazard insurance 119-120, 126
home equity line of credit 119
home inspection 115, 119
homeowners' association 51, 120, 125
homeowner's insurance 117, 120, 121
homeowner's warranty 120
HUD 49, 118-120, 128
HUD-1 settlement statement 120, 128

I

income x, 20-21, 24, 39, 40, 42, 72, 87-88, 90-92, 94, 106, 111, 113-117, 119-120, 123, 125-126
income capitalization approach 120
Internal Rate of Return 34-35, 94, 120
Internal Rate of Return (IRR) 34, 120

IRR ix, 15, 34-35, 84, 86, 91, 94, 120

J

joint tenancy 120, 127-128
judgment 48, 120
judicial foreclosure 121
jumbo loan 121

L

late charge 121
lease 5, 6, 15, 17-18, 36, 40, 85, 92-93, 117, 121, 127-128
leasehold estate 121
lease option 121
legal description 44, 121
lender 5, 7-9, 14-15, 24-26, 28, 31, 37, 41, 45, 47-48, 53, 56, 58-59, 66, 73, 78, 83, 87-88, 93, 99, 107-112, 115-119, 121-125, 127-129
liabilities ii, 8, 23-24, 36, 40, 42, 44, 66, 106, 113, 120-121, 133
liability insurance 120, 121
lien 18, 33, 39, 44, 48, 114, 117, 120-121, 127-129
line of credit 119, 122, 126
liquid asset 112, 122
loan 5, 7, 9, 13-15, 17, 21, 24, 29, 33, 47-49, 59, 61-66, 68-69, 71, 73-74, 87, 89, 111-116, 118-128
loan officer 121, 122, 126
loan origination 122, 124
loan servicer 128
loan servicing 122, 124
loan-to-value 122, 123
loan-to-value (LTV) 122
LTV 17, 21, 34-36, 69, 94, 122-123

M

market data approach 122
maturity 122
merged credit report 122
MI 123
MIP 123
modification 5, 6, 15, 19, 20, 24, 27,
     40, 55, 88-89, 93, 105-106, 122
mortgage 1, 5, 17, 21, 44, 47-48, 61,
     62, 64-65, 67, 73, 90, 111-119,
     121-129
mortgage broker 122
mortgagee 123
mortgage insurance 123
mortgage insurance (MI) 123
mortgage insurance premium 123
mortgage insurance premium (MIP)
     123
mortgagor 99, 121, 123
multi-dwelling units 123

N

negative amortization 123
net operating income 113-115, 120,
     123
net operating income (NOI) 123
net present value 123
net present value (NPV) 123
no cash-out refinance 123
no-cost loan 124
NOI 34-35, 87, 91, 113, 114, 123
non-performing 5, 15, 19, 23, 33, 55,
     66, 68, 72, 89, 105, 124
note 3, 8-9, 14, 17,-21, 23-26, 31, 36,
     39, 44, 63, 69, 71-72, 74, 77,
     88-89, 92-93, 100, 103, 105-107,

109, 111, 124, 126-127
note rate 111, 124
notice of default 8, 48, 124
NPV 123

O

original principal balance 124
origination fee 124
owner financing 124

P

partial payment 124
par value 124
payment change date 125
performing 5, 8, 14-15, 18-20, 23, 33,
     36, 55, 66, 68, 72, 89-90, 92,
     105-106, 124-125
personal property 42, 112, 119, 125
PITI 126
planned unit development 120, 125
planned unit development (PUD)
     120, 125
point 6, 28, 31, 33, 36, 37, 40, 42, 45,
     50-51, 54-55, 57-58, 69-71, 78,
     80, 90-91, 94, 101, 103, 112,
     114, 124-125
power of attorney 125
pre-approval 125
prepayment 125-126
prepayment penalty 126
pre-qualification 125-126
prime rate 69, 126
principal 5, 15, 20, 105, 111-112, 117,
     122, 124-128
principal balance 112, 122, 124-127
principal, interest, taxes, and insurance
     (PITI) 126

promissory note 126
PUD 120, 125
purchase agreement 57, 98, 102, 126

Q

quitclaim deed 115, 126

R

real estate agent 5, 117, 126-127
real estate owned 47, 66, 127
Real Estate Settlement Procedures Act
    (RESPA) 127
real property 39, 41, 44, 112, 115,
    117, 119-120, 125, 127
Realtor® ix, 127
record 41, 42, 115
recorder 114, 127
recording 48, 124, 127
refinance transaction 123-124, 127
remaining balance 62, 113, 126-127
REO iv, xi, 1, 18-19, 24, 47-50, 55-57,
    66, 68-75, 83, 107, 127
REO (real estate owned) 127
RESPA 127
right of first refusal 127
right of ingress or egress 127
right of survivorship 127

S

sale-leaseback 127
second mortgage 127
secured loan 127
security 1, 17, 21, 44, 48, 61-62, 67,
    73, 116, 122, 127-128

seller carry-back 128
servicer 58, 59, 128
services 20, 27, 34-35, 57, 64-66, 71,
    83, 85, 94, 103, 122, 128-129
servicing 122, 124, 128
settlement statement 120, 128
short sale 6, 24, 31, 49, 80, 128
subdivision 125, 128
subordinate financing 128
survey 28, 41, 43-44, 128
sweat equity 128

T

tenancy in common 128
Texas Ratio 66-71, 74, 128
title company 41, 44, 128
title insurance 18, 39-40, 124, 128
title search 99, 114, 129
transfer of ownership 129
transfer tax 129
trustee 48, 55, 57, 112, 129
Truth in Lending Act 129

U

unpaid balance (UPB) 8, 19, 70, 129

V

VA 53, 72, 115, 118-119, 129
VA mortgage 129
Veterans Administration (VA) 129

Y

yield 19, 20, 24, 91-93, 102, 106, 129

CPSIA information can be obtained at www.ICGtesting.com
Printed in the USA
BVOW050539130911

271047BV00001B/8/P